America's *First* First World War

The French and Indian War
1754-1763

D1211283

By the Same Author

Alamo Sourcebook 1836:
A Comprehensive Guide to the Alamo and the Texas Revolution
With Terry Todish
Illustrated by Ted Spring
Eakin Press, Austin, Texas, 1998

The Annotated and Illustrated Journals of Major Robert Rogers
Illustrated by Gary S. Zaboly
Purple Mountain Press, Fleischmanns, New York, 2002

America's *First* First World War

The French and Indian War
1754-1763

by

Timothy J. Todish

Illustrated with Paintings by Gary S. Zaboly,
Drawings by Joe Lee, and Map by Timothy J. Carlson

PURPLE MOUNTAIN PRESS
Fleischmanns, New York

Dedicated to John C. Jaeger, whose interest in American military history has been an inspiration to me during our lifelong friendship.

America's FIRST First World War:
The French and Indian War, 1754-1763

Second Edition, 2002

Published by Purple Mountain Press, Ltd.
1060 Main Street, P.O. Box 309
Fleischmanns, New York 12430-0309
845-254-4062, 845-254-4476 (fax)
purple@catskill.net   http://www.catskill.net/purple

America's FIRST First World War publishing history:
First edition by Dickinson Brothers, Grand Rapids, Michigan, 1982, cloth; Eagle's View Publishing Company, Ogden, Utah, 1988, trade paperback

Cover: A detail of Gary Zaboly's painting *Amherst's Review,* see page 82-83.

Library of Congress Control Number: 2002101417

Manufactured in the United States of America on acid-free paper
5 4 3

The French and Indian War
1754-1763

The French and Indian War "was destined to have the most momentous consequences to the American people of any war in which they have been engaged down to our own day—consequences therefore even more momentous than those that flowed from the victorious Revolutionary War or from the Civil War. For it was to determine for centuries to come, if not for all time, what civilization—what governmental institutions, what social and economic patterns—would be paramount in North America."

Lawrence Henry Gipson
The Years of Defeat: 1754-57 in Volume VI of
The British Empire Before the American Revolution

Table of Contents

The Scene of the Conflict
1754-1763

THE AUTHOR AT THE MAIN GATE OF FORT NIAGARA, dressed in the uniform of an officer of Rogers' Rangers. This and subsequent photos showing persons in eighteenth-century dress were taken at historical reenactments where authenticity rules are strictly adhered to, and thus they portray historical situations as accurately as it is possible to reconstruct them today. Photo by Terry Todish.

Preface to the Original Edition

THE FRENCH AND INDIAN WAR was the last in a long series of conflicts between France and England for possession of North America during the seventeenth and eighteenth centuries. Far too few modern Americans understand or appreciate the impact that this war has had on later American history.

Colonial Americans, echoing sentiments similar to many citizens of our own day, were often all too willing to let the job of defending the colonies fall upon someone else's shoulders. The members of the Massachusetts General Assembly were not unique when they observed that, "Our people are not calculated to be confined in Garrisons or kept in any particular Service; they soon grow troublesome and uneasy by reflecting on their Folly in bringing themselves to a state of subjection when they might have continued free and independent."* The obvious solution to this problem was to have Great Britain defend the colonies with her Regular troops, who apparently were thought of as being more naturally adaptable to the rigors of military discipline.

The fact that Great Britain did bear a large share of the burden of defending the colonies, both financially and in terms of manpower, would have significant ramifications in the future. Her attempt to tax the colonies to help pay for the war was one of the major issues that led to the American Revolution. Until Great Britain's final military triumph over New France, the idea of independence was unthinkable, for the French threat was considered far more dangerous and undesirable than British rule.

The French and Indian War was not only important for its political implications, it also served as a training ground for many of the military officers who would lead America to victory in the Revolution. Some of the battles, such as the Siege of

* Alberts, *Major Robert Stobo*, p. 192.

11

Fort Niagara and the Battle of the Plains of Abraham at Quebec, were executed in classic European fashion. Others were fought by new rules that made maximum use of the rugged terrain and endless forests of North America.

It may appear that I have devoted an unjustly large portion of this narrative to the exploits of Robert Rogers and his Rangers, who excelled at this type of irregular warfare. I feel, however, that this emphasis is justified for several reasons. Looked at objectively, their contribution to the final British triumph was probably greater than that of any other American unit. As a corps, they later contributed a disproportionate share of the successful leaders who served the American cause during the Revolution. Last, but not least, in spite of a growing interest in the history of Rogers' Rangers, reliable information about them is still difficult to find.

This work is not intended to be a full-length, scholarly history of the war, for others with far greater historical and literary skills have covered that ground before me. I do intend that it be a brief but accurate portrayal of the crucial events of that conflict. Through the text and the carefully selected illustrations, I hope to awaken in the reader a realistic appreciation for this colorful but often neglected period in our nation's history.

Tim Todish
Grand Rapids, Michigan
April, 1982

Private, Rogers' Rangers, 1758 issue regimental coat

Preface to the Second Edition

WHEN I first wrote *America's FIRST First World War* in 1982, my goal was to fill the need for a straightforward and easily read overview of the French and Indian War. My target market was historical reenactors, "buckskinners," and visitors to French and Indian War historic sites. Little did I realize that the book would find a much wider market, withstand the test of time, and go into a second edition in the year 2002.

Much has been learned about the French and Indian War in the past 20 years, and with this new knowledge have come new perspectives about its importance. If anything, it is now credited with an even greater role in the formation of our nation than when this book was first published. With the upcoming 250th anniversary of the French and Indian War, appreciation of its importance in American history will undoubtedly increase.

Francis Parkman's *Montcalm and Wolfe* remains a classic full-length study of the war, and it has recently been joined by Fred Anderson's *Crucible of War*. Anderson's book not only uncovers some new details about the North American conflict, but also places them in the context of worldwide events. Colonel Red Reeder's fine basic history of the war has been republished, as has John Cuneo's definitive biography of Robert Rogers. Dr. Russell Bellico, Brian Leigh Dunnigan, Lieutenant Colonel Ian McCulloch, Dr. David Starbuck, Ian Steele, Nicholas Westbrook and a host of others have contributed important new information through their research and writing. More and more primary source material from both sides continues to be published. Gary Zaboly's diligently researched artwork, supplemented by his writing talent, set the standard for artists of this era years ago, and he has now been joined by the likes of Robert Griffing, John Buxton, Joe Lee, Ted Spring and others.

While it is my intention to use much of this new information to bring the second edition up to date, I also do not want to lose sight of my original concept for the book—that it be a clear and concise, easily read overview of the war. The past 20 years have clearly shown that this is where its strength lies. This edition, with its expanded text and bibliography, will hopefully remain a foundation for readers interested in this era, inspiring further study in their areas of specific interest.

Tim Todish
Grand Rapids, Michigan
November 2001

Compagnies Franches de la Marine

Chapter One
War Comes to the Ohio Country: 1753-1754

CONTRARY to the belief of many people, America did not fight her first *World War* in the trenches of Western Europe in 1917-1918. The first world war in which America was involved was fought right here on our native soil, with an impact on our nation's history at least as significant as that of the 1917-18 war. Twenty years before the outbreak of the American Revolution, the colonies were locked in a struggle for their very existence—a struggle that rarely receives more than a passing word in modern day history books.

For some seventy-five years, France and England had engaged in a series of generally inconclusive wars both in Europe and North America. The year 1754 marked the outbreak of the last of these conflicts, which would determine once and for all which power would dominate in North America. Relations between England's King George II and Louis XV of France were already sorely strained.

A young lieutenant colonel in the Virginia Provincial Regiment provided the spark that lit the fire of what would truly be a world war, involving many of the world's civilized nations fighting in all corners of the globe. His name was George Washington. England's eventual victory in this war, known in America as the French and Indian War and in Europe as the Seven Years War, led directly to the conditions that would permit the colonies to attempt to sever their ties with the mother country in the 1770s.

Both France and England had taken an early interest in colonizing the New World, but they had gone about it in vastly different ways. New France, with its strong feudal and Roman Catholic heritage, developed along the St. Lawrence River, into the Great Lakes region, and down into the Louisiana Territory. Although French missionaries and explorers ranged far and wide, large permanent settlements were few. In the early 1750s, there were about 80,000 French inhabitants in North America, with about 55,000 of these residing in Canada. They were engaged primarily in farming and the fur trade.

England, on the other hand, had about 1,500,000 subjects in her American colonies, engaged in a wide variety of agricultural and industrial pursuits. Largely Protestant, they had become accustomed to a high degree of individual social, economic and political freedom. Although the colonies held large claims to the interior of the continent, their settled areas were primarily along the Atlantic seacoast. The Appalachian Mountains formed a natural barrier to westward expansion, but it was a barrier that was sure to fall in time. Even without the traditional rivalries between the mother countries in Europe, conflicts between the English colonies and New France were inevitable.

In the fall of 1753, Virginia's Lieutenant Governor, Robert Dinwiddie, sent Washington to warn Captain Jacques Legardeur de Saint-Pierre, the commandant of the French Fort LeBoeuf, that his post was an encroachment on the territory claimed by the colony of Virginia. Saint-Pierre received Washington and his party politely, but he paid no heed to their admonition. After a difficult journey through largely unexplored territory, Washington returned to Williamsburg to make his report on January 16, 1754.

Early the next spring, a small band of British colonists under Ensign Edward Ward began construction of a small fort at the fork where the Allegheny and Monongahela rivers merge into the mighty Ohio. In April they were driven off by a party of 500 Frenchmen, who immediately began constructing a new, larger work that they called Fort Duquesne. Lieutenant Governor Dinwiddie quickly organized an expedition of 800 men designed to expel these intruders from the Ohio Country, as it was then called. Washington succeeded to the command of this endeavor when its original leader, Colonel Joshua Fry, died after falling from his horse. The army marched without incident to the Great Meadows, about fifty miles from Fort Duquesne.

Here friendly Indians brought word that there was a small party of Frenchmen camped only six miles away. Without hesitation, Washington and forty of his men marched on the French camp, surrounding it in the dark of night. Then, in the early morning of May 28, as a light rain fell upon them, the Virginians struck the unsuspecting Frenchmen with deadly surprise. Ensign Joseph Coulon de Villiers de Jumonville, the leader of the French party, and nine of his men were killed. The rest were captured, except one who escaped to carry the news to Fort Duquesne. Washington had one man killed and two or three wounded. It is ironic that this, Washington's first battle, was also the opening skirmish in the final struggle between France and England for North America.

Captain Louis Coulon de Villiers, brother of the slain Jumonville, assumed command of a sizeable force of French and Indians at Fort Duquesne, and on June 28 marched out to meet Washington's men. Back at the Great Meadows, the Virginians threw up a small round palisade that they named Fort Necessity. Nearly surrounded by high ground, this fort was woefully inadequate. Washington's Indians, exercising what they thought was just common sense, deserted him.

The French force appeared on the morning of July 3 in the midst of a heavy rain, and the Virginians prepared for battle in the classic European fashion. The French, unfortunately, had read a different textbook. They scattered and began to fight from behind rocks, trees and bushes, Indian style. With their advantage of high ground, the French and Indians found it easy to pick off the defenders of the fort with little risk to themselves. Ironically, some of the Indians fighting with the French were from tribes that had traditionally been allied with the British—Shawnee, Delaware, and Mingoes—but who had recently been lured away by the French. Soon, nearly a third of

Washington's command was either dead or wounded, and he was forced to ask for surrender terms.

The terms offered by Villiers were generous for the most part. The Virginians were allowed to march out with the honors of war, but Washington was forced to admit in writing to the "assassination" of Jumonville. Some say that he was either accidentally or deliberately misled by his interpreter, Captain Jacob Van Braam, and did not realize what he was signing. At any rate, his first military campaign ended on anything but a successful note. Although war between France and England was not formally declared until 1756, fighting had begun in earnest in North America.

FRONTIER SETTLERS WERE OFTEN CARRIED INTO CAPTIVITY BY MARAUDING BANDS OF FRENCH AND INDIANS. Some were treated as prisoners of war by the French, but many were kept by the Indians. Some of these were tortured and killed, some were maintained as virtual slaves, and a lucky few, like John Stark, were adopted into the tribes and treated with great kindness. Tana Shoger-Vance has adopted the character of Mary Jemison, a white woman who was carried off into captivity during the French and Indian War period. Photo by the author at Fort Michilimackinac.

WOODLAND INDIAN WARRIORS USED LIGHTWEIGHT AND AGILE BIRCHBARK CANOES to traverse the lakes and rivers of the North American wilderness. Photo by the author during the filming of the History Channel series *Frontier: Legends of the Old Northwest.*

FORT NECESSITY AND THE "GREAT MEADOWS." When he first viewed the site, George Washington called it "a charming place for an encounter." No doubt his feelings changed after his humiliating defeat there. Photo by the author.

Chapter Two
Wilderness Warfare: 1755

WAGING WAR in North America was vastly different than it was in Europe. Wilderness campaigns required new methods and new thinking. Just getting an army to a place where it could fight was a monumental task, and maintaining control of the navigable waterways was of extreme importance. Although it can be said that the French probably were quicker to adapt to the rigors of forest warfare, the British were rarely as inept as their modern image pictures them to be.

Campaigns were planned on an annual basis, with little activity other than scouting and nuisance raids taking place during the winter months. In fact, much of the campaign season was lost just to raising troops, procuring supplies, and moving the armies into a position to fight. Objectives had to be won quickly, before bad weather again forced the armies back into winter quarters.

Throughout the war, British grand strategy tended to be more clearly defined and aggressive, while French strategy was more reactionary, based on what they thought the British were going to do. This was due, in large part, to the relative priorities placed on the North American war by the home governments, and is not necessarily a reflection on the ability of the military commanders.

After the fall of Fort Necessity, there was little further military action for the rest of 1754. Major General Edward Braddock of the Coldstream Guards, a veteran of over forty years' service, was made the supreme British commander for the 1755 campaign. There were four main objectives to the strategy:

1. As supreme commander, Braddock would himself lead an attack on the most difficult objective, Fort Duquesne.

2. Major General William Shirley, the governor of Massachusetts, would march against Fort Niagara on Lake Ontario.
3. Colonel William Johnson, promoted to major general for the campaign, was to lead an all-Provincial army against Fort St. Frederic, at Crown Point on Lake Champlain.
4. Lieutenant Colonel Robert Monckton would drive into Acadia, attempting to take Forts St. John and Beausejour.

Only Monckton, who captured his objectives in June, was completely successful. Shirley's Niagara Expedition was plagued with organizational problems from the start, and eventually had to be abandoned.

Elaborate plans were laid for Braddock's Duquesne Expedition. The under-strength 44th and 48th Regiments of Foot were designated to be a part of the endeavor, and sailed for America in January of 1755. Upon their arrival, they were filled up to strength with recruits from the colonies. Braddock, who was dedicated and well-liked by most of his men, worked hard to prepare his army for the task before it. Benjamin Franklin, the Postmaster General of Pennsylvania, played no small part in helping obtain enough wagons to transport the army's supplies through the wilderness. Braddock had met George Washington soon after his arrival in the colonies, and was impressed enough with the young Virginian to ask him to serve as one of his aides. Washington had hopes of earning a Regular Army commission, and he quickly accepted Braddock's offer.

When the army was finally assembled, it numbered almost 2,000 men. Nearly half were untrained recruits, a fact that proved crucial later on. Roughly a third of the total were Provincial troops, also relatively inexperienced.

Braddock's advance was cautious and conducted in good order. His pioneers, or combat engineers, hacked a twelve-foot-wide road through the virgin forest. The French watched the advance, but were reluctant to attack such a strong, well-organized column. Neither were they sure that they could defend Fort Duquesne against such a force.

By the evening of July 7, Braddock's army reached the Monongahela River at a point about ten miles from Fort Duquesne. Lieutenant Colonel Thomas Gage was ordered to take a strong advance party across the river. Almost in desperation, the French commander allowed Captain Daniel-Hyacinthe-Marie Lienard de Beaujeu to lead a force of 800 to 900 men, mostly Indians, out to meet the British advance in a last ditch attempt to save Fort Duquesne.

On the morning of July 9, Beaujeu's party ran into Gage's advance guard. It was not an ambush, as is often believed. Initially, both sides were equally surprised. The first disciplined British volleys took their toll of the French and Indians, and Beaujeu himself was mortally wounded. The French and Indians were on the verge of being routed, and a spirited British bayonet charge would probably have carried the day. Gage's men, however, failed to act aggressively. They began to waver when they had difficultly seeing their targets, who remained well hidden in the surrounding woods.

Meanwhile, the French and Indians rallied, and poured forth a deadly fire into their exposed enemy. The Indian war cries, coupled with the screams of captured British and Provincial soldiers who were being tortured before their very eyes, had an unnerving effect on the untested Regulars, most of whom had only seen garrison duty. The scene also struck terror into the hearts of the raw recruits, who were mostly colonial troops from along the seacoast, totally out of their element in the dense forest. Little by little, Gage's advance guard was driven back into the main body of the army, which had advanced to the sound of the guns. Many of the British and Provincial officers were killed or wounded. Braddock had four horses shot out from under him, and was shot through the lungs as he was mounting a fifth.

Confusion turned into panic, orders became counter-orders leading to disorder, and what had begun as an orderly withdrawal turned into a rout. In the end, 977 of the 1,459 British and Provincial troops engaged, including sixty-three of eighty-six officers, were killed, wounded or missing. Braddock lived on in agony for some time, saying to Washington before he died, "We shall better know how to deal with them another time."* He was buried in the middle of the military road, and the entire army passed over the grave so that the French and Indians would not find it.

Although Braddock is widely looked upon as being largely at fault for his own defeat because of his stupidity and stubbornness, that really is not a fair assessment. He was a European soldier of long experience, cast into a whole new realm of warfare in North America. Like nearly all of his peers, he had much to learn, but that does not mean he was stupid. His dying statement says much about the man. At the same time, his greatest success, that of getting the difficult colonial legislatures to provide the necessary support for the expedition, is largely overlooked. From a military perspective, his advance through the wilderness was generally conducted in good order and with proper security. Where it fell apart was after the initial engagement, when the French and Indians used their experience in woods warfare to terrorize and turn back the advance guard under Thomas Gage. While as overall commander, Braddock certainly must share in the blame, Gage is largely at fault for his indecisive leadership in the initial moments of crisis.

It is worth noting that George Washington, who was right there in the thick of things, never criticized Braddock. Instead, he faulted the behavior of the Regular troops under fire. Of Braddock, he said, "How little does the World consider the Circumstances, and how apt are mankind to level their vindictive Censures against the unfortunate Chief, who perhaps merited least of the blame."**

---

*May, *Wolfe's Army*, p.12.
**Anderson, *Crucible of War*, pp. 105-106.

Lieutenant Colonel Ian McCulloch gives a very fair and realistic analysis of Braddock when he writes, "The general consensus now is that Braddock's debacle was precipitated in a large part by his critical neglect on the day of battle to observe the fundamental rules of war laid down in the European manuals of the day. His leadership lapse and complacency once nearing his objective meant that his soldiers were never given a chance to demonstrate that Old World methods, properly applied, might have very well won the day." McCulloch, a former commanding officer of the Black Watch Regiment of Canada, goes on to say, significantly, that "After Braddock's defeat no inferior guerilla force would ever overcome any substantial body of British regulars during the Seven Years' War in North America."*

The defeat of Braddock's army cast a pall over the colonies, one from which it took them quite a while to recover. The partial success of William Johnson's campaign against Crown Point, or St. Frederic, helped morale somewhat. A shrewd and ambitious Irish immigrant, Johnson gained the respect and affection of the Six Nations of the Iroquois Confederacy, one of the most powerful Indian coalitions ever formed. As the King's Northern Superintendent of Indian Affairs, Johnson welcomed Indian visitors to his Mohawk Valley estate, and was honest and forthright in his dealings with them.

Johnson's all-Provincial army numbered about 3,300 men. Moving north toward Crown Point, he established a base camp at the south end of Lac St. Sacrement, which he renamed Lake George in honor of the king. The French commander, Major General Jean-Armand, Baron de Dieskau, planned to ambush the English in the woods, the same tactic that had worked so well against Braddock.

On the early morning of September 8, French forces surprised a large scouting party under Colonel Ephraim Williams of the 3rd Massachusetts Regiment, and the old Mohawk Chief Hendrik. In the desperate skirmish that followed, both Williams and Hendrik were killed and the Provincials were

*McCulloch, "Within Ourselves . . .," p. 42.

chased back to their camp. This engagement has become known as the Bloody Morning Scout.

Perhaps becoming overconfident through this easy win, Dieskau attacked Johnson's camp with his force of roughly 200 Regulars, 600 Canadians, and 600 Indians. Quickly organizing his force, Johnson repulsed several spirited attacks. Dieskau was wounded and captured, and the French eventually withdrew from the field.

As it had begun, this Battle of Lake George ended on a bloody note. Late in the day, a large party of Frenchmen were resting by a small pond when the British caught them by surprise. They were killed almost to a man, and their bodies were thrown into the pond. It has been known ever since as Bloody Pond.

With the Indian allies included, losses in the battle were about equal on both sides, with 331 for the British, and 339 for the French. Percentage-wise though, the British came out ahead, 14 percent casualties to 23 percent for the French, and they also maintained possession of the field. Johnson gave all of the captives except Dieskau to his Mohawks. While he understood that this was part of the Indian way of war, Johnson also was sensitive to European sensibilities, so tried to hide this fact from Governor Shirley.*

Johnson's Provincials could justly boast that they had met and bested a French force in the woods, a fact that helped to boost the sagging morale of the British colonists. Even so, their victory was not total. Johnson's Indians, who had served him well in the battle, now deserted him. Without their services as guides, Johnson was unable to push on to his real objective, Fort St. Frederic at Crown Point. After building Fort William Henry at the south end of the lake near the site of his battle, Johnson withdrew his forces. For his victory, he was awarded 5,000 pounds sterling and made a baronet by a grateful Parliament.

Although the year 1755 could hardly be called a success by the British, there was a bright spot on the horizon. Superior

---

*Anderson, *Crucible of War*, p. 762, n.24.

officers were beginning to take notice of a young Provincial officer who was destined to play a major part in the eventual triumph of the British cause. He was a 23-year-old captain in Blanchard's New Hampshire Regiment named Robert Rogers. The men of Rogers' company were all able woodsmen and, under his leadership, they had gained the reputation of being able to supply their commanders with reliable and much-needed information about enemy fortifications and troop movements. This was the beginning of one of the most effective fighting forces that America has ever produced—Rogers' Rangers.

The following spring Johnson authorized Rogers to raise a second Ranger company. These companies were eventually put on an "independent establishment," meaning that they were technically Regulars financed by the crown, and were not considered a part of any other regiment. This was a distinction that they enjoyed for the rest of the war. Rogers' Rangers proved to be invaluable both for their scouting prowess, and as an effective counterforce against the fearsome French Canadian irregulars, those illegal fur-traders known as coureurs de bois, and their Indian allies. The Rangers also became a formal training ground where promising young Regular and Provincial officers learned the Rangers' tactics, something that no other irregular unit on either side could officially claim.

Facing page: COLONIAL, OR "PROVINCIAL" REGIMENTS MADE UP A GOOD PORTION OF THE BRITISH ARMY DURING THE FRENCH & INDIAN WAR. Here historian and reenactor John-Eric Nelson portrays an officer in Colonel Nathan Whiting's 2nd Connecticut Regiment. Photo by the author at Old Fort Niagara.

Above: FORT JOHNSON was Sir William Johnson's second Mohawk Valley home. It was built in 1749 and was his residence during the French and Indian War years. Although not as famous as his later estate, Mount Johnson, it is a well-preserved historical attraction.

Facing page, top: FORT MICHILIMACKINAC was one of the most important of the western French posts during the French and Indian War. Located at the strategic Straits of Mackinac, it protected the French trade and supply routes to the south and west. It did not see any action in the war, but several of its inhabitants went east to fight for king and country. Among these was Charles de Langlade, one of the most notable French partisan fighters of the war. Photos by the author.

Bottom: THE FRENCH ARMY IN NORTH AMERICA consisted of a limited number of Regular Regiments. They were supported by Colonial Regulars known as the Compagnies Franches de la Marine, local militia units, the coureurs de bois (the illegal "runners of the woods"), and of course, a variety of Indian Allies. Though often outnumbered by their British foes, they generally were a brave and resourceful fighting force. Photo by the author during the filming of the History Channel series *Frontier: Legends of the Old Northwest.*

THE BATTLE DISCIPLINE AND FIREPOWER OF THE REGULAR BRITISH SOLDIER WAS AWESOME WHEN HE COULD FIGHT ON HIS OWN TERMS. Although baffled at first by the tactics employed by Indian and French irregulars, the British Regular made great strides in adapting to forest warfare under enlightened leaders such as Howe, Bouquet, and others. Massed volleys, such as the one delivered by these members of the 42nd Highland Regiment, made the difference for Wolfe's forces on the Plains of Abraham at Quebec. Photographed during the filming of the History Channel series *Frontier: Legends of the Old Northwest*.

Facing page: RANGERS SUCH AS THOSE COMMANDED BY ROBERT ROGERS AND ISRAEL PUTNAM WERE THE EYES AND EARS OF THE BRITISH ARMY, and had to be able to scout and fight in all kinds of weather. Here reenactor Paul Peterson, a retired army officer and modern day Ranger, portrays a member of Rogers' corps on a winter scout. Photographed during the filming of the History Channel series *Frontier: Legends of the Old Northwest*.

Chapter Three
The French Zenith: 1756-1757

BOTH ENGLAND AND FRANCE appointed new commanders for their 1756 North American campaigns. After considerable deliberation, King George II chose John Campbell,
the Fourth Earl of Loudoun, as his commander in chief to replace the fallen General Braddock. Loudoun was a steady soldier noted for his wide experience and administrative ability.

French commander Baron Dieskau had been captured in
the Battle of Lake George, and Major General Louis-Joseph
Gozon de Veran, Marquis de Montcalm, was appointed in his
stead. While generally perceived to be both able and popular,
Montcalm also had a dark side that would work against him.
He had a hot temper and a sharp tongue, and he often clashed
with the vain and jealous Governor General of Canada, the
Marquis Pierre de Rigaud de Vaudreuil de Cavagnal.
Unfortunately, King Louis XV had decided that the American
War was second in priority to the one in Europe, and Mont-
calm's assignment was an exceedingly difficult one.

With Montcalm came a young aide, Captain Louis-Antoine
de Bougainville, who served his country with considerable
distinction. Not all of the French soldiers, unfortunately, were
of the same quality. As Montcalm soon learned, the regular battalions in New France "had been used as a dumping ground
for the cast-offs of their parent regiments in Europe."*

In spite of Vaudreuil's considerable shortcomings, he did
understand one thing about war in North America that
Montcalm did not. He saw that while the French colonists
could never hope to meet the British on even terms militarily,
they could exploit their proficiency at la petite guerre, the
guerilla war at which the colonial troops and their Indian allies
excelled. Montcalm, on the other hand, while a very competent
general, tended to think more in terms of classic European stra-

*McCulloch, "Like Roaring Lions . . .", p. 33.

tegy, as did his Regular British counterparts. The French began 1756, which was to be their most aggressive year of the war, with a late winter expedition against the Oneida Carry, a critical portage on the water route between the Mohawk Valley and Fort Oswego on Lake Ontario. Fort Williams on the Mohawk River guarded the east end of the carry, while the west end was protected by Fort Bull on Wood Creek.

Lieutenant Joseph-Gaspard Chaussegros de Lery, a noted military engineer and an accomplished woodsman, was assigned the task of severing Fort Oswego's vital supply link to the east. He left Fort La Presentation on the St. Lawrence River with 362 men, and after a difficult two-week winter march arrived at Fort Bull on March 27.

De Lery's men captured and burned Fort Bull, but the rapid approach of a relief force led by Sir William Johnson forced the French to withdraw before capturing Fort Williams. Even so, the fall of Fort Bull left the English at Oswego in a precarious position, one that Montcalm was quick to exploit. Fort Oswego was actually three different fortifications located in close proximity to one another, controlling the juncture of the Oswego River and Lake Ontario. At this time, it was the only British post on the Great Lakes, and as such, was of great strategic importance.

Montcalm organized a sizeable force to attack Oswego, and overran it with little difficulty in August. The entire British garrison was either killed or captured. The fall of Oswego gave the French undisputed control of Lake Ontario and guaranteed the security of their supply and communication links to the west.

The faint-hearted Major General Daniel Webb compounded this disaster for the British. Rather than meeting the French threat head on, Webb withdrew all of his remaining forces from the Mohawk Valley. This left the British settlers there helpless in the face of marauding bands of French and Indians. Many of them paid with their lives for Webb's decision.

England had finally declared war on France on May 18, 1756, and George II definitely did not look upon the American theater as a low priority. The independent nature of the colonial assemblies made it extremely difficult for them to agree on anything, much less act in unison once a decision had been reached. It was hoped that Lord Loudoun would not only lead them to victory on the battlefield, but also inspire in them the intercolonial cooperation that would make final victory possible. While he was somewhat successful, at times Loudoun's typically British attitude toward authority had a negative effect on the colonists. Fred Anderson, whose book *Crucible of War* is an excellent study of relations between the colonies and the British government, notes that, "His virtually automatic response to opposition was to threaten to use force to compel submission. That tactic, while effective in the short term, tended over time to convince the colonists that Loudoun himself posed at least as grave a threat to their liberties as the French and Indians—and one much closer at hand."*

At the same time, events were occurring in Parliament that had a great impact on the conduct of the war. William Pitt was gradually gaining ground in his power struggle with the Duke of Newcastle for control of the English government. Complete victory in North America was part of Pitt's vision, and he was willing to do whatever was necessary to achieve it.

Administrative delays in England prevented Loudoun from arriving in America until late July, at which time the season was too far advanced to mount any major offensive moves for the remainder of 1756. Loudoun brought with him the nucleus of a new regiment that would become famous in the annals of American military history. Originally designated the 62nd Regiment of Foot, it was soon renumbered the 60th with a restructuring of the regiments of the army. Many of its officers were Protestant foreigners from the Dutch, Swiss, and British service. The enlisted ranks were brought up to strength by recruiting Swiss and German immigrants from the Pennsylvania frontier. Recruiting fell short of expectations, and additional soldiers had to be sent from regiments on the Irish establishment. Commonly referred to as The Royal American

*Anderson, *Crucible of War,* p. 167.

Regiment, it served with distinction in nearly all remaining major battles of the war.

When the Regular troops on both sides went into winter quarters, rugged partisan bands continued to raid and harass their enemies. On the British side, Rogers' Rangers roamed the lakes on ice skates and stalked the forests on snowshoes, scouting for days at a time without warm food or fires. Boldly they marched, taking the war to the French in all seasons and in all kinds of weather. Ranger historian Burt Loescher has rightfully dubbed them The Falcons of the Lakes.*

The Rangers brazenly raided the countryside around Forts Ticonderoga (called Carillon by the French) and Crown Point (St. Frederic to the French), even going so far as to sleep in the empty outbuildings of Fort St. Frederic. On one occasion, after making a fine meal on a captured French cow, Rogers left a note of appreciation on the horns of the carcass. Exploits such as this caused his fame to grow in the colonies and even in England, while the exasperated French put a handsome price on his head. Rogers seemed to lead a charmed life, however, and always managed to stay one step ahead of those who would bring his career to an untimely end.

It should be understood that Rogers did not invent the ranger concept. He merely refined it and brought widespread attention to it. For many years, one company of each New England Provincial Regiment had been designated as a ranging company. Rogers got his start as captain of the ranging company of Blanchard's New Hampshire Provincial Regiment. On the other side, the French colonial troops, and also the *coureurs de bois*, were also very adept at these irregular tactics.

Two things legitimately set Rogers apart from other successful partisan leaders, though. He formally trained other promising officers in his methods—he even had a Cadet Company in his corps for a time—and he set his tactics down in writing for others to study and learn from. These *Ranging Rules* are believed to be the first written military manual for irregular tactics written in North America. Rogers' tactics and

*Loescher, *The History of Rogers' Rangers*, Vol. I, p. 51.

formal training efforts were encouraged by Lord Loudoun, who himself was experienced in irregular warfare from European campaigns.

The Rangers generally tried to avoid pitched, open battles, preferring lightning-quick hit-and-run raids instead. Occasionally they were forced to meet the enemy on unfavorable terms however, as was the case on January 21, 1757. Rogers left Fort Edward on January 15, and, after picking up some reinforcements at Fort William Henry, he headed north into French territory. The force originally numbered eighty-five men, but eleven soon went lame in the bitter cold and had to be sent home.

Advancing cautiously, by the 21st the Rangers had reached a point about halfway between Ticonderoga and Crown Point. There they took up positions along the shore of Lake Champlain, hoping to ambush a French patrol or supply convoy. Two sleighs were soon observed moving north on the ice toward Crown Point. Lieutenant John Stark and twenty Rangers were ordered to head them off. Unfortunately, Stark's vision was obstructed by a point of land jutting out into the lake, and he was unable to see eight additional sleighs following the first two. Rogers sent two Rangers to alert Stark, but they did not arrive in time, and the trap was sprung too soon.

Stark's Rangers rushed out onto the ice, capturing seven Frenchmen and three sleighs, but the rest escaped. Realizing that his force was now outnumbered about two to one, Rogers ordered a quick withdrawal. The French commander, Captain Jean-Baptiste-Guillaume Le Prevost, Sieur de Basserode, correctly assessed Rogers' intentions and maneuvered his force into position to cut off the escape. Like the Rangers, the Frenchmen were hardy woodsmen, skilled in winter warfare. De Basserode's Indians were led by a famous French partisan, Ensign Charles-Michel Mouet de Langlade, from the faraway post of Michilimackinac.

The outnumbered Rangers fought like demons, but the heavy French musket fire took its toll. Rogers himself was twice wounded, once in the hand and once in the forehead. Fighting desperately to hold out until dark, the Rangers then employed the principle of one of the famous Ranging Rules that Rogers would later set down in writing. Singly or in small groups, they slipped through the French net under cover of darkness, and made their escape back up the lake.

Of the seventy-four Rangers engaged in the fight, fourteen were killed, nine were wounded, and seven were taken prisoner. Rogers estimated that he had killed 116 French and Indians, but the French admitted to only eighteen killed and twenty-seven wounded. The truth probably lies somewhere in the middle. One thing is clear; in spite being heavily outnumbered, the Rangers acquitted themselves very well.

In mid-March 1757, the French took the offensive again, moving against the under-strength winter garrison of Fort William Henry. A well-equipped force of about 250 Regulars, 950 Canadians, and 300 Indians under Captain Francois-Pierre de Rigaud de Vaudreuil, Governor Vaudreuil's brother, hoped to catch the British by surprise. Although Rigaud's force greatly outnumbered the defenders, it was mainly made up of Canadians and Indians, who lacked the temperment to conduct a formal siege. They managed to burn some of the fort's outbuildings but resolute resistance, especially by John Stark's company of Rangers, caused Rigaud to withdraw without doing serious harm. The French suffered fourteen killed and three wounded, while the British had four Regulars and three Rangers wounded. Among them was Ranger Lieutenant John Stark, who was grazed by a musket ball—the only time during his long and active military career that he was wounded.

Lord Loudoun's main objective for the 1757 campaign was the capture of the mighty fortress of Louisbourg, located on Cape Breton Island where the St. Lawrence River empties into the Atlantic. The familiar problems of supply and manpower prevented him from even arriving in Louisbourg until August. When he finally did get there, he found the fortress heavily garrisoned and supported by a strong fleet. Loudoun wisely decided to sail back to New York without risking his army.

When he realized that the bulk of the British Army was preparing to participate in a summer campaign against Louisbourg, Montcalm saw another opportunity to capture Fort William Henry. He moved up Lake George with a strong force of 6,000 French Regulars and Canadians, and some 2,000 Indians, knowing that the British lacked a sufficient force to oppose him.

On July 26, the French scored a critical victory near a spot on the lake called Sabbath Day Point. The New Jersey Regiment, or the Jersey Blues as they were more commonly known, was one of the best trained and best equipped of the Provincial regiments. A combined force of Jersey Blues and some New York Provincials were scouting down the lake near Sabbath Day Point when they were ambushed by a party of some 700 French and Indians led by Ensign Charles-Michel Mouet de Langlade. The Provincials were then pursued by Indians in canoes, and about 250 of Colonel John Parker's force of 350-400 men were killed, captured or drowned. In addition, twenty-two valuable boats were lost. Many of the prisoners were horribly tortured by the Indians. This was a loss that Lieutenant Colonel George Monro, commander of Fort William Henry, could ill afford. He had only about 1,380 men fit for duty, and General Webb sent only about 1,000 additional reinforcements under Lieutenant Colonel John Young of the Royal Americans.

This time, when the French arrived at the fort under Montcalm's personal leadership, they began a formal, deliberate siege. Although Colonel Monro pleaded desperately for help, the ever-timid General Webb refused to move from his secure position at Fort Edward, where he had about 7,000 men. Montcalm's siege tactics took their toll on the valiant garrison. Exact casualty figures are elusive. Captain John Knox states that the garrison suffered approximately 300 battle casualties. Many of the garrison were also incapacitated by disease, and at last, on August 9, Colonel Monro agreed to the terms of surrender offered by Montcalm.

The defenders were to be paroled and marched to Fort Edward under French escort. The night before the scheduled march, Montcalm's Indians, drunk on looted liquor, began to steal the captives' personal baggage. Next they fell upon the sick and wounded, killing them without mercy. Growing ever more bold, the Indians then began a general massacre of the defenseless garrison that continued until Montcalm and several of his officers, disregarding their personal safety, managed to restore order. Ian Steele, who has done the latest and probably the most accurate study of the aftermath, estimates that about 175 soldiers and ten civilians died in the unprovoked massacre, while between 300 and 500 of those captured were eventually returned, including soldiers, women, children, servants and slaves.*

In their frenzy, the Indians even dug up and scalped some of the fort's recent dead. They paid dearly for this sacrilege, for several of these dead, including Robert Rogers' younger brother Richard, had died from smallpox. The ensuing epidemic decimated Indian tribes as far west as the Great Lakes. The siege of Fort William Henry and the ensuing assault on the British captives is the basis of James Fenimore Cooper's famous novel, *The Last of the Mohicans*, which has also been made into numerous movie and television productions.

Montcalm originally planned to push on at least as far south as Fort Edward, now the northernmost fort protecting the British colonies. However, the fact that he was deserted by most of his Indians, and that he lacked the means to transport his supplies and artillery overland, would not permit this. After burning the remains of Fort William Henry, Montcalm's army retreated northward, thus ending French offensive operations for 1757. Although Montcalm had scored a tactical victory with the capture of Fort William Henry, it was not a strategic gain. The British were able to reoccupy the ground and use it as a staging area for their offensive campaigns during each of the final three years of the war.

---

*Steele, Betrayals: *Fort William Henry & the "Massacre,"* p. 121.

On the Right Flank at the First Battle on Snowshoes
Painting and caption by Gary S. Zaboly

The scene depicts the January 21, 1757, ambush of seventy-three men under Captain Robert Rogers' command by 150 French and Indians under Captains DeBasserode and LaGranville, about three miles west of Ticonderoga.

Rogers' party consisted mostly of Rangers from his own company stationed at Fort Edward. Additional volunteers came from the ranging companies of Captains Hobbs and Speakman at Fort William Henry, as well as one Regular from the 44th British Regiment.

Rogers' orders were to reconnoiter the French forts Carillon (Ticonderoga) and St. Frederic (Crown Point), both situated on Lake Champlain, and to take enemy prisoners if possible. Setting out from Fort William Henry on January 17, the expedition marched northward on the ice of Lake George, then took to the mountains and hills just west of Champlain's southern arm. On the morning of the 21st, the men arrived at a point on the lake about midway between

Carillon and St. Frederic. Here they ambushed two French provision sleighs traveling northward on the ice. Word of the Rangers' attack quickly reached Fort Carillon, however, and Rogers, attempting to return to Lake George before the enemy could intercept him, found himself ambushed as he led his men across the small valley of a frozen stream.

A crescent-shaped fusilade brought down several of the leading Rangers as the men reached the crest of the far side of the ravine. Rogers himself received a glancing head wound. Covered by volleys from the rest of his party in position on the opposite ridge, Rogers led his survivors back across the stream and there organized a stand. The fight raged for about four hours, the Rangers constantly shifting their positions to beat back the enemy's many attempts to outflank or rush them. After nightfall, Rogers and his remaining fifty-four men managed to quietly sneak around the French positions and retreat in safety to Fort William Henry. The Rangers had killed, according to one French account, nineteen of the enemy and wounded twenty-seven, of whom twenty-three eventually died of their wounds.

The picture depicts Captain Rogers holding the right flank of the crest; Lieutenant John Stark commanded the center and Ensign Jonathan Brewer the left. The Rangers around Rogers exhibit the wide array of dress typical of this period in their history, a year before the regulation green uniform was issued to them. Headgear ranged from the favored Scotch bonnet to round hats (tricorns cut down to a derby-like brim for ease of movement in the woods). Jockey caps (tricorns with just a visor in front or with attached ear flaps), as shown here on Rogers, were frequently used in the French and Indian War. Winter dress for the men was similarly varied. Blanket coats were favored, or simply blankets wrapped Indian-style around the body. Sometimes dress in the field was simply modified civilian garb: jackets, coats, flannel shirts and waistcoats.

Snowshoes, moccasins or shoes, leggings and mittens were also important items on a long winter march. Muskets, fusils or fowling pieces were sometimes sawed down for better handling, and had their barrels browned or blued to kill the sun's glint. Bullets were carried in pouches, cartridge boxes or both. Powder horns, scalping knives, and tomahawks completed the necessary weapons kit.

Used with the artist's perimission. Photo by Christopher Chadwick.

NEAR SABBATH DAY POINT ON LAKE GEORGE. In this area, a force of about three hundred and fifty of the "Jersey Blues," under Colonel John Parker, were surprised and nearly wiped out by Montcalm's French and Indians, who were on their way to victory at Fort William Henry. Photo by the author.

Facing page, top: MANY OF THE DEFENDERS OF FORT WILLIAM HENRY WERE SICK, AND NEARLY ALL SUFFERED FROM EXHAUSTION BY THE TIME THE SURRENDER TERMS WERE AGREED UPON. Harvey Anglum and Tim Carlson walk across the parade ground while other reenactors seek shelter against the walls in a scene from the History Channel series *Frontier: Legends of the Old Northwest.* Photo by the author.

Bottom: THE 60th, OR ROYAL AMERICAN REGIMENT, WAS ONE OF THE BEST BRITISH REGIMENTS TO SERVE DURING THE FRENCH & INDIAN WAR. Mike DeJonge portrays a member of one of the Light Infantry Companies, and Dr. Todd Harburn is an officer of one of the 60th's Battalion Companies. Photo by the author at Fort Michilimackinac.

A MORNING MIST HANGS OVER THE RAMPARTS OF FORT WILLIAM HENRY. The fort was built by Sir William Johnson after his victory at Lake George in 1755, and was captured by Montcalm in August of 1757. After the surrender, a large portion of the captured garrison was massacred by the French Indians. The fall of Fort William Henry is the subject of James Fenimore Cooper's tale *The Last of the Mohicans*. Photo by the author. *Below:* ROGERS' RANGERS FIRST LARGE-SCALE BATTLE TOOK PLACE IN JANUARY 1757, AND HAS BECOME KNOWN AS "THE FIRST BATTLE ON SNOW-SHOES." Here the Rangers direct their fire at French and Indian attackers. From the History Channel series *Frontier: Legends of the Old Northwest*. Photo by the author.

Chapter Four
The Tide Begins to Turn: 1758

WILLIAM PITT became Prime Minister of England in June of 1757, and although it was too late to make any plans for that season, he immediately began to plan for the 1758 campaign. His first task was to select the leaders that he felt could guide England to eventual victory. Ironically, the supreme command of the English army went to a seventy-seven-year-old Frenchman who has been called "probably the ablest general to wear a red coat between Marlborough's time and Wellington's."* Field Marshall Lord John Ligonier had fled to England at an early age to escape the Huguenot persecutions in France, and would prove to be an extremely wise choice to lead England to victory.

Lord Loudoun was recalled and his former second in command, General James Abercromby, was named commander in chief in North America. Pitt then developed a three-pronged North American strategy for 1758. His objectives were:

1. The capture of Fortress Louisbourg, which would open the way for an eventual assault on Quebec, up the St. Lawrence River.

2. The capture of Fort Ticonderoga. Located at the crucial junction of Lake Champlain and Lake George, its fall would be an important step in the invasion of Canada by the Champlain water route.

3. Another attempt to take Fort Duquesne in the Ohio Country, where Braddock had failed in 1755.

The French, on the other hand, were forced to adopt a primarily defensive and reactionary strategy. Internal corruption and two years of crop failures, coupled with the successful blockade of the sea lanes by the Royal Navy, left them no other choice.

*Anderson, *Crucible of War*, p. 215.

As usual, over the winter of 1757-58, Rogers and his Rangers remained active long after other units had either disbanded or gone into winter quarters. Before his recall, Loudoun had authorized Rogers to raise four more New England Ranger Companies, as well as one company of Stockbridge Indians, who were to serve under their own Indian officers. Loudoun had also directed that for the first time, at least officially, the Rangers were to be uniformed alike. It is probable that by the late winter of 1758, the Rangers had been issued the short green regimental coats that Rogers had ordered for them. They wore woolen or leather Indian-style leggings over their breeches, and leather shoes or moccasins protected their feet. Many types of headgear were probably worn, but the bonnet of the Scottish Highlanders was favored when it could be had. Tricorns were often cut down into round hats, and were also made into jockey, or light infantry-style caps, which were less troublesome to wear in the brush. Like their tactics, the Rangers' dress borrowed and blended the best from the regular army, the American frontier, and the native Indians.

The five new Ranger companies were ready by early March. Four were sent to serve in the upcoming Louisbourg Campaign, while one remained on the Lake George front with Rogers and the rest of his old corps. The companies under Rogers' direct command were quartered in huts on an island in the Hudson River adjacent to Fort Edward, known then, as it is now, as Rogers' Island.*

On March 10, 1758, Rogers marched out of Fort Edward into what was to be one of the most difficult battles of his career. It was a mission that he undertook with a considerable degree of apprehension. Lieutenant Colonel William Haviland,

---

*The Rangers first garrisoned this island in 1756. Contrary to what some have held, it was definitely called Rogers' Island during the French and Indian War. As one example, *The London Chronicle/Universal Evening Post* for November 23-25, 1758, reports that: "We have advice from Rogers Island, near Fort Edward, that Lieut. Holmes of the Rangers, returned the 6th ult. from a scout to Ticonderoga with about seven men; and reports, that he lay very near the fort; that there is a very large encampment there; that the enemy have erected some block-houses at their breast-work, and that many Indians are there."

the commander of Fort Edward, had sent Israel Putnam and his Connecticut Ranging Company on a scouting expedition a few days earlier. For some unexplained reason, he then publicly announced that upon Putnam's return, Rogers would be going out with 400 men. There was little doubt that this information would leak to the enemy. Yet, when the time came, Haviland reduced Rogers' strength to 180 men, less than half of what had been previously announced. The French had been trying unsuccessfully to do away with Rogers for several years, and no doubt saw this as a golden opportunity.

By March 13, Rogers and his party had advanced to within two miles of Carillon. Advised by his scouts that a combined party of ninety-six French soldiers and their Indian allies were marching down a frozen stream, Rogers quickly deployed his men for an ambush. The Rangers' opening volley killed a number of the enemy, and sent the rest into headlong flight. Captain Charles Bulkeley's Company, in hot pursuit, ran into another party of 600 of the enemy and suffered heavy casualties. Rogers quickly organized his men to repel the new threat, and the outnumbered Rangers fought valiantly for three hours. With the odds they were facing, their only hope was to hold out until dark and then disperse singly or in small groups and make their way to safety, as specified in Rogers' Ranging Rules.

One small party under Lieutenant William Hendrik Phillips, who was part Indian himself, was cut off from the main body of Rangers and surrounded. Offered good terms, they surrendered, and most of them were immediately hacked to pieces by the French Indians. Phillips was taken away to Canada, where he eventually escaped to rejoin the Ranging service.

Most of the surviving members of Rogers' party slipped through the French lines and made good their escape. Rogers himself was so closely pursued that he cast aside his green jacket, which had his commission in one of the pockets. An old legend, of doubtful veracity, claims that he used his snowshoes as skis to descend a huge rock formation and make his escape up Lake George. This rock formation overlooking Lake George is known today as Rogers' Rock. When the French found Rogers' jacket they thought that the fabled Ranger had finally met his fate, but it was not long before they realized that this was just wishful thinking.

Although Rogers made it back safely, many of his men were not so lucky. Of the 180 men engaged in the Second Battle on Snowshoes, as it is known, only fifty-four returned safely to Fort Edward. In this one tragic engagement, Rogers lost the cream of his original Ranger corps. One must seriously wonder if this might not have been the subconscious wish of Colonel Haviland, who had never really gotten along with Rogers. As for his own thoughts on the matter, Rogers merely stated, "my commander doubtless had his reasons, and is able to vindicate his own conduct."* Rogers' agony over this defeat was eased somewhat when on April 6 he received his long-awaited promotion to major. He was soon scouting and raiding up and down the lakes as before, reminding his French adversaries that he was indeed alive and well.

Command of the 1758 Louisbourg Campaign was given to two promising young colonels, Jeffery Amherst and James Wolfe. For the expedition, Amherst was made a major general, and Wolfe a brigadier.** Amherst was a meticulous organizer and not one to go into action until everything was exactly to his liking. Wolfe was also a thorough soldier, but tended to be more impetuous than Amherst. Both officers' personal bravery was beyond question, and in the ensuing campaign their personalities would complement one another beautifully. Theirs was a difficult objective, for Louisbourg was the strongest

---

*Rogers, *Journals*, p. 80.

**A brigadier in the British army of the period is not the same rank as a "brigadier general" in the modern sense. In his book *The French & Indian War* (p. 185), Colonel Red Reeder defines brigadier as "an appointment for an officer—usually an experienced lieutenant colonel or colonel—to the command of a corps consisting of several battalions, called a brigade. It is a wartime title. At the end of the war, the brigadier reverts to the ranks and title he held when he received the initial orders." Many of the promotions in North America were for this theater only, and were not permanent appointments on the Regular Army lists.

fortress in America, with four great bastions and one and one-half miles of stone walls.

Wolfe personally led a daring amphibious landing on Cape Breton Island, thus gaining a foothold for the 14,000-man army. Many of the boats used in the assault were packed so full of men that they could not be rowed and had to be towed ashore. Some, filled with members of the 78th Regiment, or Fraser's Highlanders, were shot so full of holes that the men had to plug them with pieces of their kilts just to stay afloat.*

Once the remainder of the army landed successfully, the British began a formal siege, a tactic at which Amherst excelled. It was so effective that when the French finally capitulated on July 27, 1758, Louisbourg's landward walls were severely breached and two of the giant bastions were in ruins. More than 5,000 French soldiers became British prisoners, a loss from which it would be impossible to recover. The ever-cautious Amherst elected not to follow up his victory with an immediate assault on Quebec, but the water passage had been opened, and the attack was sure to come the following year.

James Abercromby, the British commander in chief, was to lead the expedition against Carillon, or Ticonderoga, himself. Abercromby was a competent administrator, but not a highly experienced field commander. However, the second in command for the Ticonderoga expedition was a popular and dashing young brigadier whom Wolfe called the best soldier in the British Army. It was hoped that thirty-four-year-old Lord George Augustus, Viscount Howe would be the real leader of the expedition.

In early summer, Abercromby gathered his army, just over 17,000 strong, at the south end of Lake George, near the ruins of Fort William Henry. It consisted of almost 6,300 Regulars and Rangers, and 9,300 Provincial troops of varying degrees of competence and experience. While they would later be blamed for the failure of the expedition by some Regular officers, the performance of the raw colonial troops was somewhat predictable. Some of the Provincial units did not even receive their

* Harper, *78th Fighitnig Frasers*, p. 41.

muskets until three days before the army embarked, and they had almost no time to master their use or to learn the complicated military maneuvers that they would be expected to perform.*

A very unique segment of Abercromby's army was also made up predominately of native-born Americans, including many shipwrights and carpenters. Some 1,600 rugged Bateaumen, under the command of Lieutenant Colonel John Bradstreet, could not only fight, but were also charged with overseeing the transportation of the men, munitions, and supplies of the army.

Bradstreet, christened "Jean-Baptiste," was born in Nova Scotia of an Acadian mother and British father, an officer in the British 40th (Hopson's) Regiment of Foot. Bradstreet was fluent in French, and is said to have been one of the key planners behind the 1745 British capture of Louisbourg.

Earlier in the war Bradstreet had been ordered to raise his elite corps of Bateaumen, and charged with keeping open the vital supply link between Albany and Oswego. These boatmen performed their duties with great skill and daring, and it was no fault of theirs that Oswego had fallen to the French. Bradstreet is one of the unsung heroes of the war; a true logistical genius who served as Quartermaster General under both Abercromby and Amherst.

The final element of the British force was approximately 400 Mohawk warriors under Sir William Johnson, who arrived on July 7, just before the assault.

On July 5, the army embarked down the lake in what was one of the greatest spectacles ever witnessed on the North American continent. The 1,000-plus boats of the armada stretched over the lake for six miles, with Rogers and his green-clad Rangers leading the way. The bright summer sun shone on the colorful uniforms of the Regulars, Highlanders, and Provincials. Abercromby had ordered that all regimental and camp colors be left behind, but a military air was still present as the fifes played, drums beat and bagpipes wailed their

*McCulloch, "Like Roaring Lions . . ." p. 30.

ghostly melodies. Who could blame this army for feeling that it was invincible?

At Carillon, Montcalm had only about 5,000 men and two weeks' provisions. His force consisted of just over 4,200 Regulars, 450 Troupes de la Marine or Colonial Regulars, 250 Canadian Militia, and surprisingly, only 15 Indians. (Some of these troops would not arrive until the evening of July 6). Like the optimistic British soldiers, Montcalm too must have wondered if their victory was not certain.*

As expected, young Lord Howe quickly became the tactical field commander. The men, Regulars and Provincials alike, loved him. He became a good friend of Robert Rogers, scouted with the Rangers, and studied their ways. He even began to introduce their tactics and dress into the Regular regiments.

On the afternoon of July 6, Lord Howe was accompanying a party of Light Infantry and Israel Putnam's Connecticut Rangers that was trying to outflank the French entrenched camp at the portage between Lake George and Lake Champlain. They ran into an enemy patrol 350-400 men strong, under the noted French partisan Ensign Jean-Baptiste Levrault de Langis Montegron (also called Langy), and Captain de Trepezac of the Bearn Regiment. As unlikely as it might seem, this French scouting party had become lost in the woods as it returned to Carillon after watching the British advance from the top of Bald Mountain, or Rogers' Rock, as it is now known. When Langy's party unexpectedly ran into Howe's force, a brisk skirmish developed, in which the British decisively defeated the French partisans.

Captain Anne-Joseph-Hippolyte de Maures de Malartic, Adjutant of the Bearn Regiment, recorded that, "About four o'clock heard several shots and soon after a considerable firing, which we judged was directed against M. de Trepezee . . . a quarter of an hour afterwards saw some soldiers of that detachment wading towards us, and M. de Trepezee arrive

---

*Different sources give varying numbers for the makeup and strengths of both armies. For this revised edition, I have relied on those used in one of the most current studies, Lieutenant Colonel Ian McCulloch's "'Like roaring lions breaking from their chains:' The Battle of Ticonderoga 8 July 1758."

next mortally wounded, who states that M. de Langy, who was guiding them, as he was acquainted with the way through the woods, had gone astray, and did not find out his mistake until three o'clock when they undertook to cross the River of the Falls, opposite a little island, whence he was returning to the same side, on finding that there was too much water to admit of reaching the other bank; that they were attacked, on landing, by a considerable corps, and after defending themselves for some time, about 50 men escaped; that the remainder have been killed, taken, or drowned."*

Although this engagement lasted only about a quarter of an hour, its cost was incalculable to the British. As Peter Pond of the Second Connecticut Regiment later wrote, the beloved Lord Howe, "Recved a Ball & three Buck Shot threw the Senter of his Brest & Expird without Spekeing a word."** The French also realized the importance of Howe's loss when they heard of it. In his journals, Bougainville wrote, "The enemy suffered a considerable loss there in the person of Milord Howe, who was killed...He had above all in the greatest degree those two qualities of heroes, activity and audacity. He it was who had projected the enterprise against Canada, and he alone was capable of executing it."***

With the death of Lord Howe, the spirit seemed to go out of the British army, and its previous confidence evaporated. Soldiers of all ranks, and especially General Abercromby, were stunned. In addition to the death of Lord Howe, the battle was important in two other ways. British indecision gave Montcalm an extra day to strengthen his defenses, one of the key factors in the eventual French victory. However there was also a downside for the French, as this skirmish, which resulted in over 300 casualties, was the first time that they had suffered a significant defeat in the war.

It would have been a relatively simple matter for the British to take control of the narrows north of the fort, which would

Documents Relating to the Colonial History of the State of New York, Volume 10, p. 845.
**Pond, *The Narrative of Peter Pond, in Five Fur Traders of the Northwest*, p.21.
*** Bougainville, *Journals*, p. 89.

have both cut off a French escape and prevented reinforcements from reaching them. They could then have either
starved the French out, or blasted them into submission with
their siege guns. Montcalm had only about 5000 men to defend
Carillon, and a limited supply of food, so in the face of
Abercromby's much larger and well supplied army, his situation was indeed precarious.

Instead of beginning a deliberate siege, though, Abercromby ordered a massed frontal assault on the French positions with orders to carry the breastworks with the bayonet.
What was to have been a massive, coordinated attack supported by flanking artillery fire never materialized. With the
Rangers, Bateaumen and the Light Infantry leading the way,
the brave British and Provincial soldiers attacked piecemeal,
allowing the French to concentrate their fire and divert their
reserves to reinforce threatened areas of their lines. Each time
the British attacked, they suffered terrible losses. About five
o'clock in the afternoon, Captain-Lieutenant John Campbell of
Duneavis, of the 42nd Royal Highland Regiment (the famous
Black Watch) and a few of his men were able to hack their way
over the first line of French breastworks. By one report, eighteen of the Highlanders made it over the breastworks. Ten of
these survived and were taken prisoner.

It has been generally believed that Abercromby ordered the
attack without making any attempt to bring up his artillery,
and then supervised the fight from well behind the scene of the
action. Recently discovered information shows that both of
these beliefs are inaccurate. Abercromby did indeed try to con-
struct an artillery battery of three six-pound cannons and one
five-inch mortar on the south bank of the La Chute River that
would have easily enfiladed the French breastworks. However,
as the guns were being floated down the river, they overshot
the designated landing point. The boats and rafts fell under the
fire of the French guns, ending the attempt. As for
Abercromby's own position during the battle, a fresh look at an
old French map reveals that Abercromby was right behind and

slightly to the right of the attacking lines of the Royal Americans and 27th (Iniskilling) Regiment.*

By the time Abercromby finally ordered a retreat, he had suffered almost 2,000 men killed, wounded, and missing. Montcalm's casualties, while only about 550, were actually slightly greater than the British losses in proportion to the numbers engaged. The brave Highlanders of the Black Watch lost 314 killed and 334 wounded, almost two-thirds of their total strength. Their loss is "unsurpassed by any other regiment in 18th century North American warfare."**

The soldiers and Indian allies on both sides fought bravely for the cause that they believed in, and their courage and sacrifices are to be commended. Still, the reality of war is such that bravery is also accompanied with great pain and suffering, and perhaps at no time during this war was it more evident than in Abercromby's Ticonderoga Campaign. Lieutenant Archelaus Fuller, of Bagley's Massachusetts Provincial Regiment, wrote after the battle that, "The Ded men and wounded lay on the groun, the wounded having some of them legs their arms and other Lims broken, others shot threw the bodey and very mortly wounded. To hear the thar cris and se thar bodis lay in blood and the earth trembel with the fier of the smol arms was a mornfullous as ever I saw."***

Among the casualties of the Royal Highland Regiment was their Major, Duncan Campbell of Inverawe, whose death has sparked an interesting legend. Although the names were changed, Campbell's story was immortalized by Robert Louis

---

*The plan to establish the artillery battery was rediscovered by Nicholas Westbrook, director of Fort Ticonderoga, while doing research at the Huntington Library in California. He also discovered a letter that stated that Abercromby "came up with the Highlanders, " who were last in the order of march. Lieutenant Colonel Ian McCulloch, CD, of the Canadian Armed Forces, and formerly the commanding officer of the Canadian Black Watch Regiment, noticed the map notation about Abercromby's position during the attack. See "'Like Roaring Lions Breaking from Their Chains': The Highland Regiment at Ticonderoga," compiled and edited by Nicholas Westbrook, in *The Bulletin of the Fort Ticonderoga Museum*, Volume XVI, Number 1, 1998, pp. 65-67 for Abercromby's position during the battle, and pp. 83-87 for the attempt to establish the artillery battery.

**McCulloch, "Like Roaring Lions . . .," p. 73.

***Fuller, *Journal*, p. 11.

Stevenson in his poem *Ticonderoga: A Legend of the West Highlands*, and it is also well documented in other sources.

Years earlier, at Inverawe, his home in Scotland, Campbell had been confronted by a stranger who begged him for sanctuary, claiming that he had just killed a man in a fair fight. Campbell agreed to shelter the man, but was then astounded to learn from the man's pursuers that the victim of the killing was Campbell's own cousin. Campbell denied any knowledge of the killer, but had difficulty sleeping that night, torn between his loyalty to his cousin and the promise he had made to shelter killer. Later that night he awoke from a fitful sleep to see his cousin's ghost standing by his bed. A hollow voice said, "Inverawe! Inverawe! Blood has been shed. Shield not the murderer!" The next day he tried to get the murderer to leave, but the man reminded Campbell of his oath. Hoping to arrive at a compromise, Campbell led the man to a nearby cave. That night the ghost again appeared and offered the same admonition. The next morning Campbell went to the cave, but the man was gone. The ghost appeared again on the third night, this time warning, "Farewell, Inverawe! Farewell, 'till we meet at Ticonderoga!"

Duncan Campbell had come to America with his regiment, not yet knowing the meaning of the word Ticonderoga. The French called the strategic post between Lake Champlain and Lake George *Carillon*, but the traditional Indian name for the site was *Ticonderoga*, and this is the name that the British adopted. Campbell told many people of his amazing experience, and as Abercromby's campaign took shape, many of his brother officers realized the significance of their destination. It is not known if Campbell realized that Carillon was "Ticonderoga," but his brother officers tried to shield Campbell from that knowledge. It is known that Campbell tried to sell his commission before the campaign, but Loudoun would not let him.* On the night before the battle the ghost appeared in Campbell's tent. That morning he announced to his friends, "He

---

* Pargellis, *Lord Loudoun*, p. 313.

came to my tent last night! This is Ticonderoga! I shall die today."

Campbell's arm was shattered by a French bullet during the attack, and he was carried back to Fort Edward. He died there on July 17 and is buried in a cemetery just north of the present-day village of Fort Edward.*

Although the accomplishment was largely overshadowed by Abercromby's disaster, the British did win a significant victory in August of 1758, when Lieutenant Colonel John Bradstreet captured Fort Frontenac, situated on the northeast corner of Lake Ontario. The capture of Frontenac not only severed a vital French supply link between the forts in the Ohio Country and those in Canada, it also helped to restore a little British pride and confidence. And it was done without the loss of a single life.**

The British scored another victory at the Battle of Fort Anne in early August.*** Rogers and eighty of his Rangers were part of a mixed force of about 700 that had been searching the area of Wood Creek northeast of Fort Edward for enemy patrols. These French and Indian partisans had ambushed a supply convoy and killed not only the military escort, but also a number of women and children. It had been a quiet scouting expedition and 150 of the men had already been sent back to Fort Edward by August 8. That morning, Israel Putnam's Connecticut Rangers were leading the column, and Rogers' men were in the rear. As they marched along, an Indian suddenly appeared from nowhere, grabbed Putnam, and carried him off before his men could react.†

A sharp fight broke out up and down the line. Because of

---

*Francis Parkman, *Montcalm and Wolfe*, pp. 635-637. This version of the Campbell legend, including the direct quotes, is taken from Parkman. Stevenson's poem is available from many sources. This and other versions of the legend closely parallel Parkman's account.

**Anderson, *Crucible of War*, p.264.

***Fort Anne was an old fort that had seen service in earlier French and Indian Wars, but was nothing but ruins by 1758. It played no part other than lending its name to the nearby engagement. Today all that remains of the fort is a portion of the well, located in a parking lot.

†Many historians have blamed Rogers for allowing the British to be surprised on that day. They claim that he gave away their position by engaging in a shooting contest with a British officer, which was contrary to his own regulations. I have read numer-

the thick underbrush, it took Rogers and his men about a half-hour to advance into a position where they could engage the enemy.

Just as he arrived on the scene, Rogers spotted a huge Indian struggling hand to hand with an officer of Gage's Light Infantry. Rogers took careful aim with his musket and shot the Indian cleanly through the head. The Indian's body was later measured at 6'4", a giant of a man for those days.

The firing eventually slackened and the French withdrew, leaving the British in possession of the field. Forty-nine British and Provincial soldiers were killed, and about seventy-seven French and Indians. Although not of major importance, the Battle of Fort Anne was a heartening English victory nonetheless.

Putnam was carried into Canada and eventually exchanged. He was reportedly saved from Indian torture by the French partisan, Lieutenant Joseph Marin de La Malgue. Both were Masons, and when Putnam made the "grand hailing sign of distress," Marin intervened at great risk to his own personal safety.

Command of the Fort Duquesne Expedition was entrusted to a reliable Scotsman, Brigadier John Forbes, who was originally trained as a medical doctor. Backing him up were Colonel Henry Bouquet, a talented Swiss mercenary serving in the Royal American Regiment, and George Washington of the Virginia Provincial Regiment. Although suffering from a painful illness, Forbes approached his task with vigor and enthusiasm. About 1,400 Regulars and 5,000 Provincials were assigned to the expedition.

Forbes felt that the greatest error Braddock made was his failure to build strong base camps along his line of march, providing him with secure positions to fall back on in case of a temporary setback. Determined not to repeat the error, Forbes

ous firsthand accounts of this battle, and there seems to be substantial evidence that this is true.

Another question also comes to mind. Israel Putnam was an experienced and competent Ranger officer. As the leader of the march that day, why did he not have an adequate advance guard and flanking parties that would have given him warning of this ambush?

took the time to build a series of forts along his route, culminating with the formidable Fort Ligonier about fifty miles from Duquesne.

Forbes' strategy was to prove its worth. As the army neared Fort Duquesne, Major James Grant was allowed to move ahead with 800 men in an attempt to take the fort in a surprise night attack. Grant's men became lost in the woods and were attacked and routed by the French. Although they suffered 300 casualties, the survivors managed to fall back to the base camp at Fort Ligonier, which Bouquet successfully held.

Despite Grant's temporary defeat, Forbes pushed ahead confidently. Seeing this, the French burned and abandoned Fort Duquesne and retreated to Fort LeBoeuf. On November 25, 1758, Forbes marched his army into the ruins of the once mighty Fort Duquesne and held a service of thanksgiving.

Forbes left Bouquet to build a new and even stronger fort at the forks of the Ohio, which he named Fort Pitt in honor of the Prime Minister. Forbes returned to Philadelphia, where he soon died of his illness. Washington returned to his home in Virginia, and did not reenter army life until seventeen years later, when another cause beckoned him.

Even though he did not destroy the opposing French army, Forbes' victory was a tremendous accomplishment. The logistical problems he had to overcome just to reach Fort Duquesne were awesome, and the smoothness with which his cosmopolitan army operated was a tribute to his leadership and that of his senior officers.

The year 1758 did not end well for New France. Louisbourg, Frontenac, and Duquesne all had fallen. These were important strongholds in the east, middle and west of the French colonial empire. Communication and trade between Canada and the French possessions in Louisiana were severely handicapped, and the outlook for the coming year was not much better. Montcalm had sent his trusted aide Bougainville back to France to plead for more men and supplies. When he made his appeal to Colonial Minister Nicolas-Rene, Comte de

La Ferriere Berryer, Bougainville was told that, "When the house is on fire, one cannot occupy oneself with the stable." To this Bougainville replied, "At least Monsieur, nobody will say that you talk like a horse."*

Meanwhile, Pitt had decided to recall the unlucky Abercromby and make Jeffrey Amherst commander in chief in America for the 1759 campaign. Calm and deliberate, even considered slow by some, Amherst would prove that he was capable of leading England to decisive victory over the French.

Amherst was a man of high principle, even to the point of stubbornness. In his book *Chronicles of Lake Champlain*, Dr. Russell Bellico gives a thoughtful analysis of Amherst's abilities. He notes that Amherst saw many British defeats in his early years. He was promoted from colonel to major general without having much experience in independent command, which may account for his deliberate planning to insure every chance of success. Bellico goes on to say, "Although not as dashing as some other contemporary generals, Amherst had a laudable military career during the French & Indian War, characterized by unbroken successes. Amherst left nothing to chance; his methodical, careful management of campaigns resulted in few casualties, no setbacks, and ultimate victory in North America."**

Amherst held a low opinion of Indians, but was respected and even well liked by his soldiers. Major Alexander Campbell, of the 77th Highland Regiment, wrote on June 19, 1759, "Our General is beloved by his soldiers, Honoured and Esteem'd by his officers, Carful of mens lives and healths, in short he is the man I would choose to serve under of any I know in the service."***

*Windrow, *Montcalm's Army*, p. 28.
**Bellico, *Chronicles of Lake Champlain*, p. 117.
***Richards, *The Black Watch at Ticonderoga*, p. 30.

CHRIS MATHENEY PORTRAYS MAJOR ROBERT ROGERS in the History Channel series *Frontier: Legends of the Old Northwest*. Photo by the author at Fort DeChartres.

Below: THE SECOND BATTLE ON SNOWSHOES, OR THE BATTLE OF ROGERS' ROCK. In March of 1758, Rogers' Rangers engaged in one of their fiercest battles against a band of seasoned French partisans just a short distance from Fort Ticonderoga. Here the Rangers are desperately trying to regroup and fight off their French attackers in a scene from the History Channel series *Frontier: Legends of the Old Northwest*. Photo by Jean Roberts.

MONUMENT TO ROGERS' RANGERS ON ROGERS' ISLAND. Rogers' Rangers lived in huts on the island, located in the Hudson River adjacent to Fort Edward. The island also housed a barracks complex and a military hospital. The monument was erected in 1964 by the late Earl Stott, who then owned the portion of the island where the Rangers encamped. The Island's current owner, Frank Nastasi, hopes to rebuild some of the historic structures and establish a museum dedicated to Rogers' Rangers and the other British soldiers who were stationed there. Photo by the author.

Above: MIKE DEJONGE AND JERRY OLSON PORTRAY MEMBERS OF THE LIGHT INFANTRY COMPANIES OF THE 60th, OR ROYAL AMERICAN REGIMENT during the filming of the History Channel series *Frontier: Legends of the Old Northwest.* The British high command hoped that the Light Infantry would eventually replace the Colonial Rangers, but it never happened. Photo by the author.

Facing page, top: FROM THEIR QUARTERS ON ROGERS' ISLAND AND AT FORT WILLIAM HENRY, ROGERS' RANGERS VENTURED FORTH IN ALL KINDS OF WEATHER to gather information for their British superiors. Here the author, Paul Peterson, and Jim Sisk march through the snow in a scene from the History Channel series *Frontier: Legends of the Old Northwest.* Photo by Mike DeJonge.

A VIEW OF ROGERS' ROCK FROM THE WATERS OF LAKE GEORGE. According to legend, Rogers' descended this treacherous precipice on his snowshoes in order to escape from the French and Indians who were closely pursuing him. Photo by the author.

LORD GEORGE AUG-UST, VISCOUNT HOWE, WAS ONE OF THE MOST COMPETENT BRITISH OFFICERS TO SERVE IN NORTH AMERICA. His death in the opening stages of the 1758 campaign against Fort Ticonderoga played a major part in the disastrous British defeat. Here Mike DeJonge portrays Lord Howe for the History Channel series *Frontier: Legends of the Old Northwest*. His hair is cut short, and his uniform is modified in the way that Howe ordered for campaigns in the wilderness. Photo by the author.

Facing page, top: THE SOUTH WALL AND ENTRANCE TO THE "PLACE D'ARMES" AT FORT TICONDEROGA. Called "the Key to a Continent," Ticonderoga was successfully defended by Montcalm in 1758, but was taken by Amherst the following year. Photo by the author.

Bottom: THE MIGHTY FORTRESS OF CARILLON, OR TICONDEROGA, viewed from Mount Defiance, or Rattlesnake Mountain. Rogers' Rangers and other British spies often observed French activities from this vantage point. Abercromby's assault of 1758 never reached the stone walls pictured here. The fort was not as complete as shown here, and the attack was directed at French earthworks constructed about one half mile away, to the left of the area shown in this photo. Photo by the author.

WHEN THE BRITISH ATTACKED FORT TICONDEROGA, MONT-
CALM'S SOLDIERS FIRED FROM BEHIND HASTILY CON-
STRUCTED WOODEN BARRICADES. *Below:* THE BRITISH DEATH
TOLL IN THE ATTACK ON THE FRENCH LINES AT TICON-
DEROGA WAS STAGGERING. The brave men of the Royal High-
land Regiment lost nearly two thirds of their strength, and casualties
in other units were also very high. Both photos by the author, during
the filming of the History Channel series *Frontier: Legends of the Old
Northwest.*

THE GRAVE OF MAJOR DUNCAN CAMPBELL OF THE 42ND HIGHLAND REGIMENT. Campbell was wounded in the assault on Ticonderoga and died a short time later at Fort Edward. He was the hero of a famous and well-documented ghost story immortalized by Robert Louis Stevenson in his poem, *Ticonderoga: A Legend of the West Highlands*. Photo by the author.

FORT LIGONIER, in Pennsylvania's beautiful Laurel Mountains, was the last strong base camp built by Forbes during his Fort Duquesne Expedition. The fort was successfully defended by Bouquet's men on October 12-13, 1758, after Grant's disastrous defeat. In this picture, members of the recreated Royal American Regiment from Fort Pitt participate in the annual Fort Ligonier Days, commemorating Bouquet's successful defense of the fort. Photo by the author.

THE RED GOLIATH: THE BATTLE NEAR FORT ANNE, AUGUST 8, 1758, by Gary S. Zaboly. This painting captures the moment when Rogers' Rangers, after struggling through the heavy underbrush, finally arrive on the scene of the fighting. Rogers spies a huge Indian locked in hand-to-hand combat with an officer of Gage's Light Infantry, and dispatches him with a shot through the head. Photo by the artist and used with his permission.

Chapter Five
Montcalm, Wolfe & Amherst
A Year of Heroes: 1759

BOUGAINVILLE returned to Canada with only 400 Regulars for reinforcements. As 1759 dawned, the Marquis de Montcalm had only a total of 3,500 Regulars and 14,500 colonial troops with which to defend all of New France. He decided that his best course of action would be to leave Colonel Francois-Charles de Bourlamaque at Carillon with a small force, and concentrate the bulk of his army at Quebec. He hoped that the British would again get such a late start that he could avoid any major battles until bad weather forced the enemy back into winter quarters. If he did have to give up Quebec and Montreal, Montcalm intended to withdraw down the Mississippi River to Louisiana.

British grand strategy for 1759, once again, had three main objectives:

1. Major General Jeffery Amherst would attempt to capture Ticonderoga, the site of Abercromby's humiliating defeat a year earlier, and then push on to Montreal.

2.Brigadier John Prideaux and Sir William Johnson would first retake Fort Oswego, and then move on to capture Fort Niagara.

3. Major General James Wolfe would sail up the St. Lawrence River to take Quebec.

In addition, in order to safeguard last year's gains, Brigadier John Stanwix was sent to reinforce and strengthen Fort Pitt at the Forks of the Ohio.

It should be noted that Montcalm had earlier came up with a very imaginative offensive plan for 1759. He proposed to invade the Carolinas from the sea with a force of 4,000 men, and then drive north, splitting the British colonies in two. He counted on the Quakers of Pennsylvania to remain neutral, and also hoped for support from some of the German colonists and the Cherokee Indians. This daring plan was originally approved, but then later scrapped for lack of money.

Amherst was determined that his 1759 Ticonderoga Campaign would not be another debacle like Abercromby's. He assembled his army at the head of Lake George, near the site of Johnson's 1755 victory over Dieskau, and established a strong base camp that he called Fort George. His position now secure, Amherst moved down the lake in boats, with the Rangers again leading the way. This year, however, poor weather prevented another spectacular scene like the one of 1758.

The Rangers landed near Ticonderoga and drove off what little French resistance was there to meet them. The rest of the army landed safely and Amherst began to methodically position his guns for a formal siege. As he did so, Rogers brought word that the French had totally abandoned the outerworks where Montcalm won his victory the year before. Bourlamaque had decided that he could not withstand a lengthy siege by a strong and determined foe. Rather than risk being trapped at Ticonderoga, he planned to withdraw to St. Frederic while he still could, leaving Captain Louis-Philippe Le Dossu d'Hebecourt and 400 men behind to delay Amherst.

On the night of July 26, Rogers was sent on a critical mission with sixty men in three boats. They were to try to cut a log boom that the French had built across the narrows of Lake Champlain, in order to keep the British from getting beyond them to cut off their retreat. As the Rangers were sawing on the boom, the desperate French were lighting the fuses to several mines that had been set inside the fort. Hebecourt was planning to flee northward with his rear guard, hoping to leave the British with nothing but a pile of ruins. Amherst learned of these plans from French deserters, but was unable to convince any of them help try to extinguish the fuses.

Suddenly, a deafening roar broke the stillness of the summer night, and in the flash of the explosion, the Rangers working on the boom caught a glimpse of Hebecourt's fleeing men. Rogers, reacting with his typical quickness and daring, ordered his men to lift their boats over the boom and give chase. Although heavily outnumbered, the aggressive Rangers were able to force ten of the French boats aground on the east shore of Lake Champlain. The occupants escaped into the woods, but the next day the British recovered large amounts of munitions, military stores, and personal baggage from the grounded boats. Thus the mighty fortress of Ticonderoga fell into British hands at last. In face of the much lighter French resistance this year, it took only four days to accomplish. Contrasted with the heavy British losses of 1758, by Amherst's count in 1759, only sixteen men were killed, fifty-one wounded, and one was reported missing.*

The retreating French stopped at Crown Point only long enough to blow up Fort St. Frederic. They then fell back to Isle aux Noix, ten miles down the Richelieu River, and dug in there.

On August 1, Lieutenant John Fletcher of Rogers' Rangers brought word to Amherst that St. Frederic had also been blown up and abandoned. Amherst ordered Captain Moses Brewer and 200 Rangers to march ahead and hold the ruins until the main army could advance. Arriving at Crown Point himself on August 4, Amherst immediately began construction of a new and stronger fort. It would share with Fort Pitt the distinction of being the two largest and strongest British forts in North America. Never again would the French and their Indian allies threaten New York and the New England colonies through the Champlain Valley.

One cannot help but speculate how the course of the war might have been altered if Robert Rogers had been allowed to implement a plan he had advocated for the winter of 1757-1758. He had proposed to skirt Carillon and capture St. Frederic in a surprise move, arguing that this would be a relatively easy task due to the weak and unsuspecting winter gar-

*Bellico, *Sails and Steam*, p. 93.

rison. Carillon, also garrisoned with just a skeleton force, could then have been squeezed and starved into submission before good weather allowed the French to send adequate reinforcements. Lord Loudoun later recorded in his personal diary that he did not approve Rogers' proposal because it would have interfered with his own plans for the conquest of the Champlain Valley. *

Rogers' Rangers were now called upon by Amherst to show their talents in a new and unusual area. Amherst wanted a road to connect the Champlain Valley with the New England colonies. It would not only serve a military purpose; it would also open the route for future trade and travel. John Stark, now a captain, was ordered to take 200 Rangers and build a road from Crown Point to Fort No. 4 on the New Hampshire border. It is difficult to pinpoint the exact starting and completion dates for this road, but it appears from entries in Amherst's journal that it was begun about August 8 and completed about September 9. The construction of this seventy-seven mile road through the wilderness in roughly a month's time is an accomplishment of which the Rangers could be justly proud.

As Amherst was moving on Ticonderoga, Prideaux was advancing toward Oswego. Occupying it without a struggle, he left Lieutenant Colonel Frederick Haldimand with a strong force to cover his rear. Prideaux then moved on toward Fort Niagara, at the strategic junction of the Niagara River and Lake Ontario. Although Niagara was an old fort, it had been significantly strengthened by its current commander, experienced engineer Captain Pierre Pouchot, of the Bearn Regiment. The fort was well supplied and garrisoned by about 600 men.

Prideaux's siege got off to a rather shaky start. Due to the inexperience of his engineers, one of the first gun emplacements, erected under the cover of darkness, was found to be facing 180 degrees from where it should have been. Such minor obstacles were quickly overcome, and the British began to slowly but surely tighten the net around Niagara.

British fortunes took a tragic turn when General Prideaux

---

*"I am bound to do this as he will break into my plan for taking Ticonderoga if the frost permits." Entry in Lord Loudoun's diary for January 13, 1758; quoted in Loescher, *The History of Rogers' Rangers*, Volume 1, p. 223.

was accidently killed in a mortar mishap. Captain John Knox later recorded in his journal that he was "unfortunately killed in the trenches, on the evening of the 19th, by an accident, the Gunner inconsiderately firing, as the General was passing; the shell burst as soon as it had cleared the mouth of the cohorn, •a small mortar] and a large piece of it struck him in the side of his head."* The expedition's second in command, New York Provincial Colonel John Johnston, fell soon thereafter. He was killed by a musket shot while inspecting the progress of the siege works.

Command then fell on the shoulders of Sir William Johnson. Johnson had more experience in dealing with Indians than he had as an active soldier, but he conducted the siege with remarkable skill. He had made considerable progress in reducing the fort when his scouts brought word that a 1,300-man French relief force was approaching. This party was under the command of Captain Charles-Philippe Aubry and Captain Francois-Marie Le Marchand de Lignery.

Johnson's force consisted of some 2,300 soldiers plus a number of friendly Indians. If the relief force got through to Pouchot, it would alter the numerical balance considerably. In a bold and skillful move, Johnson withdrew the majority of his men from the siege lines. He ambushed the French relief force a short distance from the fort at a place called La Belle Famille, and decisively defeated it. He then returned his men to the siege lines before Pouchot's defenders knew they were gone.

Johnson called for a parley and advised Captain Pouchot of this turn of events, demanding that he now surrender the garrison. Skeptical of the story, Pouchot sent one of his officers to Johnson's camp to obtain confirmation. Any doubts were dispelled when the French observer was shown the sixteen officers of the relief force who had been captured, including Aubry and Lignery. Pouchot formally surrendered Fort Niagara on July 25, and the French lost yet another important link between Canada and their western territories.

Wolfe left Louisbourg for Quebec in early June with a force

*Knox, Volume I, p. 510.

of about 8,500 men, mostly Regulars. His appointment to lead the Quebec Expedition had not been welcomed by everyone in the government, but he was determined to succeed. When the Duke of Newcastle complained to the king that Wolfe was mad, the king replied, "Mad is he? Then I hope he will bite some of my other generals."* Frail and sickly at thirty-two years of age, James Wolfe was totally dedicated to his profession. He was generally disdainful of the Provincial troops, and he held an even lower opinion of Indians. Wolfe strictly forbade "the inhumane practice of scalping, except when the enemy are Indians."**

Assisting Wolfe were Brigadiers Robert Monckton, George Townsend, and James Murray, all good soldiers in their own ways, although they did not necessarily always see eye to eye with Wolfe. Especially valuable was the chief naval officer of the expedition, Vice Admiral Sir Charles Saunders. Although rarely recognized, the supremacy of the Royal Navy played an important part in the eventual victory at Quebec, as well as the war as a whole. During the siege of Quebec, 277 English ships crossed the Atlantic in support of the army, while not a single French ship did so successfully.***

Many of the participants in the French and Indian War gained their greatest fame in later pursuits. George Washington led the Continental Army to victory in the Revolutionary War, and then served his new nation as its first President. John Stark, Israel Putnam, Horatio Gates, and Richard Montgomery all became famous American generals, and many others served with distinction in varying capacities during the Revolution. William Howe, Lord George Howe's younger brother who commanded the Light Infantry at Quebec, became the British commander in chief during the Revolution. Admiral Saunders had a young sailing master in his command at Quebec by the name of James Cook. On the French side, Louis-Antoine de Bougainville was both Montcalm's friend and one of his best officers. Shortly after the war, Bougainville transferred to the navy for health reasons.

* May, *Wolfe's Army*, p. 25.
**Wolfe, *Instructions to Young Officers*, p. 89.
*** Harper, pp. 40-41.

Both he and Cook later gained their greatest fame as navigators and explorers of the vast uncharted areas of the Pacific.

Montcalm was expecting Wolfe's arrival, for Bougainville had returned from France with a captured letter detailing the enemy's plans for the expedition. The British received similar intelligence help from two officers who had recently been held prisoner in Quebec, and who were able to provide Wolfe with up-to-date information about the city's defenses. Major Patrick Mackellar, Wolfe's chief engineer, was captured in the fall of Fort Oswego in 1756. Major Robert Stobo, of the Virginia Provincial Regiment, had been given up as a hostage (along with Captain Jacob Van Braam) at Fort Necessity. This was to ensure that some French prisoners who had been sent back to Virginia would be released, as called for in the terms of the capitulation.

One of these French prisoners, the partisan Michel La Force, was considered such a valuable catch that, on Stobo's own advice, the Virginians declined to release him. As a consequence, Stobo remained in French custody, and several times risked his life by sending valuable military information to his British contacts. He recently had made a daring escape from Quebec and joined Wolfe's expedition, sharing the valuable information he had accumulated during his captivity.

British fortunes took a turn for the better on the 18th of July, when a portion of their fleet managed to slip by Quebec's defenses and get upriver from the city. Young James Cook was instrumental in taking the soundings of the St. Lawrence River that allowed British ships to anchor in the Basin, and then later safely pass above the town. This exposed the French to danger from a side they had not prepared for, and positioned the British astride their only supply routes to Trois Rivieres and Montreal. The subsequent British raids on the Canadian countryside forced the French to alter their defenses and put a further drain on their already limited manpower. On September 5, this naval presence was augmented by Brigadier Murray and a strong land force.

On June 26, 1759, Wolfe occupied the Isle of Orleans, located in the St. Lawrence River a few miles northeast of the main city. Here he established his base camp and began to implement plans for the siege.

On the night of June 28, the French attempted to destroy the British fleet by using fireships. Their plan failed when overzealous crewmen set the ships afire too soon, giving the British enough warning to permit them to take evasive action.

On the 30th of June, Monckton captured Point Levis, only one mile from Quebec. From this commanding position, the British artillery was able to rain a deadly fire down on the city.

The French failed in a desperate attempt to retake Point Levis on July 12. Then Wolfe took the offensive again on July 31, with an amphibious assault on the French lines at Montmorency, along the Beauport Shore east of the walled city. Just as had happened at Ticonderoga in 1758, rather than a coordinated assault, orders were disobeyed and the attack was made piecemeal without proper support. The brave British force stormed ashore in disorganized waves. Those who made it through the withering French fire then had to struggle across an exposed mud flat just to reach the heights to be scaled. As the first redcoats began to pull and crawl their way to the top, a sudden thunderstorm drenched everything and sent them sliding back down. Watching the assault from the deck of a ship, Wolfe had his cane carried away by a cannonball. Finally seeing that it was hopeless, he ordered a retreat. The British suffered 440 casualties while the French had not lost a man.

As early as July 19, Wolfe had proposed to attack the town from about three miles to the west, from a point called St. Michel. When he discovered that the place was well defended, he dropped the idea. On September 10, he took his brigadiers to survey a spot called Anse du Foulon (now Wolfe's Cove), where he felt that the heights leading to the Plains of Abraham could be successfully scaled. In spite of his subordinates' apparent lack of enthusiasm, Wolfe decided that he was going to follow through with his plan.

At 1:30 a.m. on September 13, the final steps of Wolfe's plan were put into operation. Diversionary troop movements, which had been going on for several days, were intensified. At 2:00 a.m., the initial assault force of 1,700 men climbed silently into smaller boats from the troop transports.* Two more waves soon followed. The second also disembarked from the transport ships, while the third wave waited on the south side of the river, across from Anse du Foulon, to be ferried across by the same small boats when they became available.

The Light Infantry of Lieutenant Colonel William Howe overshot their intended landing spot by about 150 yards, but by sheer determination, quickly scrambled up the heights. They routed a small guard stationed at the top by attacking it from the rear, and secured the ground while the main part of the army landed. By the time the morning fog lifted, 4,500 British soldiers were deployed in line of battle across the Plains of Abraham.

Both commanders were now in difficult positions. Once he gained the Plains of Abraham, Wolfe wanted to lure Montcalm out to engage him in a classic European-style battle, but unless and until that happened, his men were dangerously exposed. Deadly French artillery and sniper fire forced the British officers to direct their men to lie flat on the ground until the order to advance was given.

This may have caused it to appear from Montcalm's vantage point that the enemy had already dug in. At any rate, the French general decided to attack right away, rather than give the British time to strengthen and reinforce their positions and bring up artillery. Montcalm began his advance at about 10 o'clock in the morning. He has been criticized for this decision over the years, mainly because Bougainville was only about one and one-half hours away with an additional 3,000 men. As it was, Montcalm marched out to attack with a force about

---

* A popular legend has it that Wolfe, riding in one of the first boats, was contemplating his chances of success and brooding over the words of a line in one of his favorite poems. He confided to an aide that he would rather have written that particular line than take Quebec. From Thomas Gray's *Elegy Written in a Country Churchyard*, the line declared that, "The paths of glory lead but to the grave." (Parkman, *Montcalm and Wolfe*, p. 539).

equal to Wolfe's 4,500 men, but many of the French were Militiamen rather than Regulars.

The French army advanced, some in column and some in line formation, while the British line, stretching for a full mile, was in ranks three deep. The French began to fire at 200 yards. The British, showing tremendous fire discipline, waited until, as British army historian Sir John Fortescue wrote, "Thirty-five yards only separated the opposing arrays, when the word rang out, the still red line sprang into life, the recovered muskets leaped forward into a long bristling bar, and with one deafening crash, the most perfect volley ever fired on [a] battlefield burst forth as if from a single monstrous weapon, from end to end of the British line."* The effect was devastating, opening huge gaps in the French lines. The initial volley was followed by approximately six minutes of disciplined platoon firing. When the smoke cleared, it revealed that the French lines had broken, and the British commenced a fearsome bayonet charge. The Highland troops dropped their muskets and charged forward in a frenzy, screaming and slashing with their broadswords.

Many of the French ran pell-mell for the city gates, but some of the Militia and their Indian allies stayed on the field and skirmished with the British Regulars. During this stage of the battle, which lasted approximately two hours, Wolfe's men also came under the fire of the French artillery. It was during this time that the British suffered most of their casualties.

Wounded three different times, Wolfe died content in knowing that the French were on the run. Montcalm was shot through the body as he rode back to the city, and he died early the following morning knowing that both Quebec and New France were now certainly lost.

Governor Vaudreuil took most of the remaining French troops and fled toward Montreal. Approaching Quebec from the east, Bougainville correctly read the situation and retreated to Point aux Trembles, a safe distance west of the town. Captain Jean-Baptiste-Nicolas-Roch de Ramezay, left in com-

* Fortescue, *History of the British Army*, p. 381.

mand of the small garrison in the city, formally surrendered Quebec on September 18.

Although the war dragged on for another year, the fate of New France was no longer in doubt. Considering the importance of the victory, the cost was remarkably small. The British had fifty-eight killed and 600 wounded, while the French lost 500 killed and 350 captured. Regrettably, many of the wounded of both sides died over the winter in a city that had virtually been reduced to rubble and had little ability to give them shelter or proper care.

GENERAL JEFFERY AMHERST (Dr. TODD HARBURN), RANGER CAPTAIN JOHN STARK (DAVE FAGERBERG), AND TIM R. TODISH AS AN OFFICER OF RANGERS are shown in this scene from the History Channel series *Frontier: Legends of the Old Northwest.* Photo by the author.

THE FRENCH "CASTLE" AT FORT NIAGARA was built to look like a chateau to deceive the Indians, but was heavily fortified. It is the oldest building still standing at Fort Niagara, which was a military base from the time it was built by the French in 1726 through the 1960s. Photo by the author.

THE REMAINS OF FORT GEORGE, Amherst's base camp for the 1759 Ticonderoga Expedition, can be seen in the Lake George Battlefield Park, Lake George, New York. Photo by the author.

Amherst's Review
Painting and caption by Gary S. Zaboly

In early September 1759, at Crown Point, General Jeffery Amherst, 42, reviews his army outside the walls of the huge new English fort, under construction, one month after the French evacuation of the Point. Major Robert Rogers, 27, accompanies the General as he begins inspecting Rogers' elite Ranger corps.

On the left, a squad of Rangers decked out in field gear will soon be leaving on a scout into the no-man's land to the north. Beyond the squad, a detail of Stockbridge Indian Rangers stands with rested firelocks.

A Ranger adjutant also inspects the line, which includes a mastiff scout dog trained not only to hunt down the enemy, but also to attack and maim him. One of the huskier Rangers presents a blunderbuss, a favorite weapon for skirmishing on the lakes in whaleboats, bateaux or canoes.

Despite Regular Army orders, the dress of His Majesty's Independent American Rangers was not always uniform. Money was difficult to come by to outfit the new recruits and everything from headgear to arms depended to a great extent on availability. Green, however, was the preferred color of the uniform of most of the companies under Rogers' direct command. Typical frontier hunting garb may have been preferred for long stints in the brush.

Whaleboats mounted with wall-pieces and protective shields wait to be filled by Rogers' Rangers for the big raid on St. Francis. Whaleboats assigned to each regiment had been ordered to be so designated with the number or name of the regiment painted on the bows.

In the left middleground, a company of the 1st Royal Regiment stand with shouldered arms while, beyond them stand soldiers of the New Jersey Blues. To their right are grenadiers of the 27th Iniskilling Regiment, Colonel William Haviland's own.   General Amherst's horse is held by an aide, while officers of the Provincial and Regular troops ponder a plan of the fort's current condition.

The fort itself is being fronted with squared pine logs. Before it, unseen behind the earthen glacis, is a ditch fifteen feet deep which surrounds the entire fort; artistic license has removed part of the wooden wall to show the earth that was used to pack the cribbings. A glimpse of one of the stone barracks can be seen beyond the main gate.

Fort St. Frederic, the considerably smaller French structure, is in a state of semi-ruin in the distant background. The narrow neck of Lake Champlain stretches beyond, and on the horizon, are the Green Mountains of Vermont.

From the author's collection; used with the artist's permission.

CROWN POINT was of strategic importance to both the French and the British during the French and Indian War, and at different times both sides fortified the spot. Viewed through the remains of the main gate, the ghostly shell of the British soldiers' barracks serves as a silent reminder of the courage of the soldiers who battled there over two hundred years ago. The ruins of the French Fort St. Frederic can be seen nearby. Photo by the author.

Chapter Six
The St. Francis Raid:
September–November 1759

O N SEPTEMBER 13, the day of Wolfe's victory on the Plains of Abraham, Robert Rogers was embarking from Crown Point on the most difficult mission of his career, a raid on the Abenaki village of St. Francis, or Odanak as the Indians called it. For years, the Abenakis had ravaged the New England frontier. Sweeping down from their home on the St. Francis River, near its junction with the St. Lawrence, they had killed hundreds of settlers and carried countless others off into captivity. In fact, the current chief of the village, Joseph Gill, was the son of two British captives who married after being adopted into the tribe. Although they were considered to be Christianized Indians by their French allies, they did not let religion interfere with their methods of waging war.

The capture of two British officers, supposedly on a mission seeking peace with the Indians under a flag of truce, prompted General Amherst to issue Rogers orders to destroy the Abenaki village. However, there is strong evidence that these officers were using the flag of truce as a ruse to safely get through to Wolfe at Quebec with dispatches from Amherst. If true, their capture was fair play. The British had, on other occasions, detained French parties who came to their posts under similar pretenses when their true purpose was obviously to gather intelligence.

Regardless, this was a raid that Rogers had been itching to make for years, and now that the time had come, he was ready. "Remember the barbarities that have been committed by the enemy's Indian scoundrels...Take your revenge....[but] it is my orders that no women or children are to be killed or hurt."*

*Rogers, *Journals*, p. 145.

So read Amherst's orders to Rogers. The purpose of the mission was clothed in secrecy to conceal the Rangers' true objective. Everything at Crown Point was designed to appear normal to any French or Indian spies who might be watching. Connecticut Provincial Robert Webster recorded in his journal that "Stil at Crownpint this Day the Scout Seat out for Suagothel 500 in No. they Took 30 Days Provision with them under the Command of majer Rogers."*

Shortly after dark on the 13th, a mixed force of about two hundred Rangers, Regulars and Provincials headed north in 17 whaleboats. Rowing all night, by dawn Rogers' party reached the mouth of the Otter River. Hiding their boats, they slept during the day, keeping a watchful eye for French patrols on the lake. They continued traveling at night and hid during the day as they moved north into French territory. On the fifth day, an accidental gunpowder explosion wounded several men. The injured and some other men who had become ill, forty men in all, were sent home to Crown Point. This was twenty percent of Rogers' force.

On September 23, the tenth day after leaving Crown Point, the party reached Missisquoi Bay at the northeast end of Lake Champlain. Here the Rangers hid their boats, with enough food for the return trip stored in the lockers. Two trusted Stockbridge Indians remained hidden nearby, with orders to catch up to Rogers if the boats were discovered by the enemy. Then the men began the 100 mile march to St. Francis, through country that few living British colonists had ever seen.

Captain John Stark, one of Rogers' closest friends and ablest officers, was conspicuously absent from this expedition. Although no official explanation is known to exist, other than that he was building the road to Fort No.4, it was perhaps Stark's wish that he not be included. On April 28, 1752, while on a hunting trip with his brothers and two other men, Stark was captured by a party of Abenaki Indians from St. Francis. He was taken back to the village and forced to run the gauntlet; that is, to run through a double row of Indians armed with

*Robert Webster's *Journal*, entry for September 13, 1759.

sticks and clubs, who struck and beat him mercilessly until he reached the far end of the line. Given a ceremonial pole with which to defend himself, Stark did not submit meekly. Rather, he took the offensive and swung his pole viciously while running down the line. This and other acts of bravery gained him the respect of his captors, and thereafter he was well treated until he was ransomed by agents of the Massachusetts Bay Colony later that summer.

During his time in captivity, Stark gained valuable knowledge of the territory around St. Francis, which he almost certainly provided to Rogers before the expedition. It is very possible that he chose not to accompany the expedition himself because he had developed a genuine affection for some of the tribe during his captivity. In his later years, Stark often said "that he had experienced more genuine kindness from the savages of St. Francis, then he ever knew prisoners of war to receive from more civilized nations."[*]

Leaving their boats behind, the raiders now began a miserable nine-day march through the drowned lands, a seemingly endless swamp north of Missisquoi Bay. Marching through water a foot or more deep, the Rangers were forced to tie their moccasins to their feet to keep from losing them. At night, they would fashion platforms in the trees in which to sleep.

On the evening of their second day in the swamp, the Indians who had been left to guard the boats came in and announced that they had been discovered by a party of 400 Frenchmen and Indians. Realizing that he could not now return by the same route, Rogers sent Lieutenant Andrew McMullen back to Crown Point with a message for General Amherst. After striking St. Francis, the Rangers would march south and east to the Connecticut River, and then follow it down to Fort No. 4. Knowing that they would be desperate for food, Rogers instructed McMullen to have supplies waiting for him at the junction of the Connecticut and Wells rivers.

Ten days after leaving their boats, the party reached the St. Francis River about fifteen miles above Odanak. The river was

*Caleb Stark, *Memoirs of John Stark*, p. 15.

about five feet deep and very swift, and the Rangers had to form a human chain in order to get across. Rogers now had 142 men left with which to attack St. Francis.

Under cover of darkness, Rogers took Lieutenant George Turner of the Indian Company, and Ensign Elias Avery of Fitche's Connecticut Provincial Regiment to scout the town. They found that the Indians were engaged in a "high frolic or dance."* At 3 o'clock in the morning, Rogers moved his men to within 500 yards of the town, deploying them on all sides to be sure that none of the occupants would escape.** They struck at the first light of dawn, catching the weary Abenakis by surprise. As they charged into the village, the Rangers saw "about six hundred scalps, mostly English" hanging from poles by the lodges.*** As the groggy Indians stumbled out of their dwellings they were shot, tomahawked or bayoneted. Many of the Indians were trapped inside their burning buildings, making it impossible to get an exact count of the casualties.

Rogers estimated that about 200 Abenakis were killed in the swift and brutal action, while French and Abenaki estimates of the casualties are far lower. It is not known how closely Amherst's order against harming women and children was adhered to, but about twenty-five were taken prisoner. Five of these turned out to be adopted white captives. These white captives, plus three Indian girls and two young boys, were chosen to accompany the Rangers on their return. The rest of the survivors were turned loose with a stern warning from *Wobi Madaondo,* or "the White Devil," as the Abenakis called Rogers.† If the St. Francis Indians ever again dared to raid the British colonies, Rogers would return, and the next time there would be no survivors!

*Rogers, *Journals,* p. 146.
**Calculated from the information in Rogers' *Journals,* the date of the attack would have been October 6. Rogers states that they arrived at St. Francis on the evening of the 22nd day after their departure from Crown Point, which is known to have been September 13. (Rogers, *Journals,* p. 154) In other sources, the date of the attack often varies slightly, most commonly being given as October 4. The Indian monument at St. Francis lists the date as the 4th, and Gary Zaboly, who has done a considerable amount of research on it, also believes that the 4th is correct.
***Rogers, *Journals,* p. 154.
†Loescher, *The History of Rogers' Rangers,* Volume II, p. 4.

By 7:00 a.m. it was all over. The Rangers gathered up what food was available, then burned the rest of the village. According to Rogers, one Stockbridge Indian had been killed and seven men were wounded, including Captain Amos Ogden, of the Jersey Blues, who was shot through the body. With 500 or more French and Indians in the area looking for them, there was no time to waste. Leaving Odanak in ruins, Rogers' men marched along the St. Francis River for several days, then turned south towards Lake Memphremagog. In spite of his serious wounds, Captain Ogden was able to keep up with the column.

By the time the party reached Lake Memphremagog on October 13, their food was almost gone. They were still about 100 miles from where Amherst was to have supplies waiting, if Lieutenant McMullen had gotten through with the message. Over Rogers' objections, an officers' council voted to break up into nine small groups, in the hope that the hunting would be better. Rogers agreed reluctantly, knowing that the small groups would not stand a chance if they were overtaken by the pursuing French.

As Rogers feared, the French caught up with at least two of the small groups. On October 15, seven men of Ensign Elias Avery's party were captured. Two of these later escaped and caught up to Rogers, telling him that the French were in almost as bad a shape as he was, and that they were about ready to give up the pursuit. The second group was made up of the parties of Lieutenant James Dunbar, of Gage's Light Infantry, and Lieutenant George Turner, traveling together. Twenty men in all, they were caught in a surprise dawn attack, and ten of the men and both of the officers were killed.

The weather turned cold and rainy, adding to the Rangers' misery. On October 20, the starving men of Rogers' own party finally reached the Connecticut River, but they were still 60 miles from where they hoped to find food. They covered this distance in only three days, making remarkable time for men in their condition. As it turned out, Lieutenant McMullen *had* gotten through, and Amherst *had* arranged to have the food waiting at the rendezvous. However, Lieutenant Samuel Stephens, commander of the relief party, had waited at the spot only two days. Hearing the guns that the approaching Rangers were firing as a signal, Stephens feared that he was about to be attacked by the French, so he headed back down the Connecticut River to Fort No. 4 with the much needed food. Rogers' men arrived on the scene only to find the still-smoking remains of Stephens' fires. Rogers later wrote, "Our distress upon this occasion was truly inexpressible, our spirits greatly depressed by the hunger and fatigues we had already suffered…"*

Despite the seeming hopelessness of the situation, Rogers quickly regained control. Leaving Lieutenant Grant in command of the remainder of the party, Rogers, Captain Ogden, a Ranger, and one of the Indian boys started down the river on a hastily built raft. Before he left, he promised the starving men that he would have food back to them in ten days.

Rogers started down the river on October 27, and the next day he and his men lost the raft, and nearly their lives, at the White River Falls. Too weak to cut logs for a new raft, they had to burn them to the proper lengths. They knew that if anything happened to this raft, they would never be able to build another.

They reached their last obstacle, the Wattaquitchy Falls, on October 30, and successfully lowered the raft over the raging water. They continued down the river, now so hungry and weak that they had to tie themselves to the raft to keep from falling off. Finally, on October 31, they arrived at Fort No. 4. Food was immediately dispatched to the remainder of the party, and it reached them just as Rogers had promised—the tenth day after he left on the raft.

Since leaving St. Francis, Rogers had lost three officers and forty-six men. Seventeen had died as a result of enemy action and thirty-two of starvation. Only two of those captured are known to have survived. For his deplorable conduct at the

*Rogers, *Journals*, p. 155.

Wells River, Lieutenant Stephens was court-martialed and cashiered from the service. All of New England rejoiced that St. Francis had finally been destroyed. A contemporary newspaper reported that, "A just Providence never designed that those bloodthirsty Heathen should go down in the Grave in Peace."*

N.B. For a more detailed account of Rogers' St. Francis Raid, including reprinted primary accounts from both sides, see this author's annotated and illustrated (by artist/historian Gary Zaboly) edition of Robert Rogers' *Journals*, also published by Purple Mountain Press.

ON THE WAY TO ST. FRANCIS, ROGERS' MEN HAD TO CROSS THE TREACHEROUS ST. FRANCIS RIVER BY MAKING A HUMAN CHAIN. The river today is much slower and more shallow than it was in 1759. Photo by the author during the filming of the History Channel Series *Frontier: Legends of the Old Northwest.*

*Cuneo, *Robert Rogers of the Rangers*, p. 114.

MEMORIAL TO THE INDIANS WHO DIED IN ROGERS'
RAID ON ODANAK or ST. FRANCIS. The original village
was destroyed in the raid of October 1759, which was immortalized by Kenneth Roberts in his novel, *Northwest Passage* and
by the movie of the same name. Today there are monuments, a
museum, and a Catholic Chapel on the Abenaki Reservation. It
is located just north of Pierreville, Quebec, and is open to visitors. Photo by the author. The inscription reads:

NEMIKWAIDAMNANA
"WE REMEMBER"
This area is planted as a
living memorial to the
SAINT FRANCIS INDIANS
Men, women and children
Who died in Rogers' Raid
October 4, 1759

THE RETURN MARCH FROM ST. FRANCIS WAS A LIVING NIGHTMARE, with bad weather and lack of food added to the threat of attack by pursuing parties of French and Indians.

Facing page, top: BANDS OF INDIANS AND FRENCH WHO PURSUED ROGER'S MEN AFTER ST. FRANCIS eventually did catch several of the small parties, inflicting heavy losses.

Bottom: A COUNCIL OF RANGER OFFICERS MAKES PLANS FOR THE RETREAT AFTER THE ATTACK ON THE ABENA-KI VILLAGE OF ST. FRANCIS. Photos by the author from the History Channel series *Frontier: Legends of the Old Northwest.*

FORT No. 4, so called because it was in Township No. 4 of the Massachusetts Bay Colony, was built by civilian settlers in the area about 1744. Rogers floated down the Connecticut River on a raft to this post after the St. Francis Raid, and from here food was sent back upriver to his starving men. The current reconstruction of the fort is located near Charleston, New Hampshire. Photo by the author.

JOHN JAEGER PORTRAYS AN OFFICER OF ROGERS' RANGERS, AND DR. TODD HARBURN AN OFFICER OF THE 60th, OR ROYAL AMERICAN REGIMENT, in this scene at Fort Michilimackinac. Photo by the author.

Chapter Seven
The Fall of New France: 1760-1763

ROGERS' RAID on St. Francis not only put an end to the Abenaki threat, it also warned all other French-allied tribes what would happen to them if they continued to fight. Most decided to stay neutral during the 1760 campaign. The other British victories in 1759 assured that the conquest of New France would most certainly be completed the following season.

General Francois-Gaston, Duc de Levis, Montcalm's deputy, was now the military commander. Seizing the initiative early in 1760, he launched an attack on Murray's under-strength winter garrison at Quebec. Levis hoped to retake Quebec before the spring thaw allowed the British to send adequate reinforcements. In April, he managed to lure the British out onto the Plains of Abraham. Both armies were about 3,800 strong, but half of Murray's men were either sick or still recovering from wounds from the previous year.

The two commanders found their positions almost exactly reversed from Wolfe's siege a year earlier. After more than an hour of heavy fighting, Levis had outmaneuvered Murray's smaller force, and could have decisively crushed it had not one of the senior French officers failed to promptly follow Levis' orders. The French lost fewer men, and also captured some of the light British artillery. The British, however, simply fell back inside the walls of the city and, lacking heavy siege artillery, Levis was unable to do them further harm. When the British fleet returned on May 9, the French were forced to withdraw to Montreal.

Amherst's strategic plan for 1760 was to capture Montreal in a three-pronged move:

1. Brigadier Murray's army would move up the St. Lawrence River from Quebec.

2. General Amherst would go west to Lake Ontario, then move down the St. Lawrence to Montreal.

3. William Haviland, now a brigadier, would move north down the Champlain Valley and Richelieu River.

While Haviland was readying his small army for the invasion of Canada down Lake Champlain, Rogers and his Rangers participated in two notable engagements. On June 5, 1760, they met and defeated a force that outnumbered them almost two-to-one in the Battle of Point Au Fer, at the northwestern end of Lake Champlain. Then, in a daring move, on June 15 they captured Fort St. Therese, located between the French posts at St. Johns and Chambly on the Richelieu River. Remaining hidden until the gate opened to let in a hay wagon, the Rangers then rushed from cover and captured the fort without loss of life on either side. After burning Fort St. Therese and a nearby village, the Rangers rejoined Haviland's army.

As things developed, Haviland's army met the bulk of the French resistance. On the 11th of August, Haviland's 3,400-man force started north from Crown Point. Rogers and his Rangers, 600 strong, led the way. On August 15, they spearheaded the attack on Isle aux Noix's fortified positions commanded by Bougainville. Along with some of Colonel John Darby's Light Infantry, the Rangers carried three light field pieces through the forest until they could be brought to bear on several French warships that were anchored in the Richelieu River. When the British guns opened fire, the ships tried to flee down the river. One was forced aground and captured by a group of Rangers who swam out to it. Abandoned by his naval support, Bougainville had no choice but to fall back to St. Jean, a move that he accomplished in a difficult night march.

In an August 17 entry in his journal, Provincial lieutenant Thomas Moody recorded an engagement involving a British radeau, which was basically floating artillery barge. It shows that the naval engagements of the war were every bit as deadly and terrible as the land battles, "one of the Ruddos was Order'd to cover the Grenigers [grenadiers] who went to Land one [on] the Point opposit to the Fort. [Isle aux Noix] A Shot which was the Second that was sent from the Enemy Capt Legg of the Royal Artillery both his Leggs Shot off died soon After. Christopher Langley the Calf of his leg shot away. Nathaniel March both of his Legs. James Urin of our Company shot off by the Knee. The Amputation was above. Robert Towerson the top of his knee which was Amputated."*

Haviland pursued the French relentlessly, forcing Bougainville to fall back again and again. From St. Jean, the French retreated to the old fort at Chambly, and from there they united with Bourlamaque's army along the St. Lawrence River near Montreal.

Murray and Haviland were now close enough to support one another if need be, but they decided to wait for Amherst before making their final move on the French. Amherst had left Oswego on August 10 with over 10,000 soldiers and 700 Indians. After capturing Fort Levis (Ogdensburg, New York) on the way, he joined up with Haviland and Murray on September 6. In the face of this British advance, the beleaguered remnants of the French army consolidated in Montreal.

Amherst encircled and prepared to lay siege to the city, which had little in the way of real fortifications. He outnumbered the defenders about 18,000 to 2,100.

Appraising his situation realistically, Governor Vaudreuil knew that he had no chance. He drew up a list of fifty-five proposed terms of capitulation. Bougainville carried them to Amherst, who agreed to some of the terms, modified others, and rejected a few that were totally unacceptable. One request he flatly refused to consider was that the French be allowed to surrender with the honors of war. In direct reference to the fate of the garrison of Fort William Henry, Amherst cited "the infamous part the troops of France have acted in exciting the savages to perpetuate the most horrid and unheard of barbarities in the whole progress of the war..."** Amherst stood firm in

*Moody, *Diary of Thomas Moody*, p. 26.
**Parkman, *Montcalm and Wolfe*, pp. 597-598.

the face of French pleas that he relent, and on September 8 Vaudreuil surrendered all of Canada to the British. Before the formal surrender, the Chevalier de Levis ordered his proud battalions to burn their regimental colors rather than let them fall into the hands of the British. Although the European war would drag on for another three years, the struggle in North America was finished.

It is worth noting that of the approximately 18,000 troops who accepted the surrender of Montreal, fewer than 11,000 were British Regulars. Over 6,500 were Provincials, and there were also more than 700 Indian allies. After over five years of fighting in North America, in terms of uniforms, weapons and equipment, the British Regulars bore more resemblance to the Provincials and Rangers than they did to their fellow Regulars serving in the European theater.*

Amherst had one last job for Robert Rogers and his Rangers, those intrepid soldier-woodsmen who contributed so valuably to the British triumph. Rogers and two Ranger companies under Moses Hazen and Joseph Waite were to have the honor of going west to accept the surrender of Fort Detroit and the other western French posts.

After a difficult journey through country that few, if any, British subjects had ever seen, Rogers' party took possession of Detroit at the end of November. From there he sent Lieutenant John Butler and a small force to occupy Forts Miami and Ouiatenon (Fort Wayne and West Lafayette, Indiana, respectively), while he started north toward Fort Michilimackinac (Mackinaw City, Michigan) himself. Bitter winter weather forced Rogers' party to turn back; the job would have to be completed the following spring. Rogers returned to New York City, arriving on February 14, 1761. He fully appreciated the momentous events that he had participated in, as he explained in his *Journals*, published in 1765:

> "Thus, at length, at the end of the fifth campaign, Montreal and the whole country of Canada was given up, and became

*Anderson, *Crucible of War*, p. 410.

subject to the King of Great Britain; a conquest perhaps of the greatest importance that is to be met with in the British annals, whether we consider the prodigious extent of country we are hereby made masters of, the vast addition it must make to trade and navigation, of the security it must afford the northern provinces of America, particularly those flourishing ones of New England and New York, the irretrievable loss France sustains thereby, and the importance it must give the British crown among the several states of Europe: all this, I say, duly considered, will, perhaps, in its consequences render the year 1760 more glorious than any preceding."*

The war officially ended with the Treaty of Paris in 1763, and the French danger to the British colonies was over. Also in 1763, a serious threat by the Eastern Indians died with the failure of Pontiac's uprising.

There was, however, another more ominous threat on the horizon. It was a situation that a few farsighted Englishmen, and even some Frenchmen, anticipated long before. The colonists, always of an independent nature, now felt it safe to assert themselves even more. Britain's attempts to make the colonies help pay for the late war, just or unjust as they may have been, were met with strong opposition in America. The British Redcoat, so recently the hero of the day, would soon become a hated symbol of oppression. But that is another story for another day . . .

*Rogers, *Journals*, pp. 195-196.

FORT CHAMBLY was one of a line of posts built to protect Canada from a British invasion down the Champlain Valley and Richelieu River. The first log fort was constructed on the site in 1665. British forces under Haviland captured it in 1760 and then went on to join Murray and Amherst at Montreal, whose fall spelled the end of New France. Photo by the author.

Facing page, top: THE SURRENDER OF THE FRENCH FORCES AT MONTREAL on September 8, 1760, marked the end of the fighting in North America. Photo by the author at the Feast of the Hunter's Moon, at Fort Ouiatenon, West Lafayette, Indiana.

Bottom: THE SITE OF FORT ST. THERESE ON THE RICHELIEU RIVER is marked by a stone monument. The fort was captured in a daring raid by Rogers' Rangers in 1759. Photo by the author.

Rogers at Detroit, 1760
Painting and caption by Gary Zaboly

The last expedition of Major Robert Rogers in the French and Indian War began on September 12, 1760, when, at recently surrendered Montreal, he received secret orders from General Amherst. These directed him to take 200 Rangers, in fifteen whaleboats, westward along the St. Lawrence River, and across lakes Ontario and Erie to Detroit. Not only would Rogers accept the surrender of that distant French trading post, but he would also relieve the garrisons of the other French forts on and near the lakes, and make peace with the various Indian tribes of the vicinity, as well as carefully document his passage for the benefit of future English expeditions.

Reaching the western end of Lake Erie on November 20th, Rogers sent forward emissaries to announce his arrival and his terms. The French commandant of Detroit, Captain Bellestre, according to local Indians who greeted Rogers, "had set up an high flag-staff, with a wooden effigy of a man's head on the top, and upon that a crow; that the crow was to represent himself, the man's head mine, and the meaning of the whole, that he would scratch out my brains. This artifice, however, had no effect; for the Indians told him (as they said) that the reverse would be the true explanation of the sign."

Indeed, Captain Bellestre peacefully surrendered Detroit on November 29th; the garrison was disarmed and later sent as prisoners to Fort Pitt. Among the Indians who had formerly been allied with the French was the Ottawa, Pontiac, and with him several other chiefs. Rogers conferred to assure them of the peaceful intentions of the English in the region. The Canadians who owned farms surrounding Detroit were allowed to remain, as long as they swore an oath of allegiance to England.

Major Rogers is depicted a couple of days after the surrender. His silver-laced officer's jacket of wool, lined with green serge, includes cording on his right shoulder as rank designation, button-loops, and white metal buttons. Such a decorated uniform would undoubtedly have been worn only on formal occasions. A black ostrich feather decorates his green-painted leather cap. Red garters tie his green ratteen leggings. His arm cradles a fusil, and a cutlass hangs at his side.

In the middleground, Rangers remove trade goods from their

whaleboats. Bad weather is approaching, and worsening conditions will force Rogers, on December 16th, to abandon a side-trip from Detroit intended to receive the surrender of faraway Fort Michilimackinac. Parties sent to relieve other French posts were more successful.

Rogers made the report of his journey to General Amherst at New York on February 14, 1761. At 29 years of age, he was one of the true heroes of the five-year conflict for control of North America (and certainly its most energetic); though in his later years he continually strove to revive the great fame he had once enjoyed, it would sadly forever remain for him an elusive objective.

Epilogue

The fall of New France gained Great Britain a new empire of tremendous size and wealth. Even at this early date, however, many astute observers were questioning whether she would be able to hold on to the prize. Ironically, Montcalm himself saw this situation clearly, and during the Siege of Quebec he wrote:

"M. Wolfe, if he understands his trade, will take to beat and ruin me if we meet in fight. If he beats me here, France has lost America utterly: yes, and one's only conclusion is, in ten years farther, America will be in revolt against England!"*

*The Marquis de Montcalm, August 24, 1759 as quoted in Barney, Flowler, *The Adirondack Album*, Volume Two, p. 29.

THEN AND NOW. Historical reenacting is a wholesome and rewarding activity with something to offer every member of the family. Reenactors work hard to master their craft so that they can properly interpret history for the public. At the same time, reenactors have the opportunity to do things that most people can only dream of, such as staying at historic sites and taking part in the filming of historic movie and television productions.

The author's son Tim R. Todish started reenacting literally as an embryo, and has been involved ever since. In the left photo, he is seen in September 1981, at age four, outside the Water Gate of Fort Michilimackinac. The right photo was taken inside the stockade at Fort Michilimackinac in August of 1997. A veteran of the 1991 movie *The Last of the Mohicans*, Tim here is being coached by Producer/Director Gary Foreman just before being chased down and tomahawked by Indians during the 1763 attack on Fort Michilimackinac. The scene is for the "Pontiac" episode of the award-winning History Channel documentary series *Frontier: Legends of the Old Northwest*. Both photos by the author.

ONE OF THE ADVANTAGES OF BEING A HISTORICAL REENAC-
TOR is having the opportunity to participate in events like the Fort
Ticonderoga Military Tattoo and getting to work with groups like the
"real" Black Watch. Here Kelly, Flossie, and Amy DeJonge pose with
Private Jamie Henderson, Lance Corporal Andrew Lambert, and
Private Stewart Paton of the Pipes & Drums of the Black Watch in
July 1997. Photo by the author.

ONE OF THE AUTHOR'S PROUDEST MOMENTS AS A REENAC-
TOR was at the 1995 Fort Ticonderoga Military Tattoo, when I was
invited to march with the color guard of the U.S. Army's 75th Ranger
Regiment. Photo by Joan Ryskamp.

Facing page, bottom: IN JULY 1997, THE PIPES AND DRUMS OF THE
42nd ROYAL HIGHLAND REGIMENT, OR THE BLACK WATCH
AS IT IS OFTEN CALLED, RETURNED TO FORT TICONDEROGA,
the scene of one of the most important battles in their long and hal-
lowed history. They also participated in the dedication of a new
memorial cairn honoring the members of the regiment who lost their
lives there on July 8, 1758. Photo by the author.

Selected Bibliography

The purpose of this bibliography is twofold: to list the major sources consulted in the preparation of this book, and also point out to the interested reader where to find more in-depth information on specific topics of interest. In some cases, more than one edition of a particular title is noted.

Alberts, Robert C. *The Most Extraordinary Adventures of Major Robert Stobo.* Houghton Mifflin Company, Boston, 1965.

Amherst, Major General Jeffery, J. Clarence Webster, editor. *The Journal of Jeffery Amherst: Recording the Military Career of General Amherst in America from 1758 to 1763.* University of Chicago Press, Chicago, and Ryerson Press, Toronto, 1931.

Amherst, Major General Jeffery and Colonel William. *Journals of Major General Jeffery and Colonel William Amherst, 1758-1760.* Reprinted in Volume III of *An Historical Journal of the Campaigns of North America for the Years 1757, 1758, 1759, and 1760,* by Captain John Knox. The Champlain Society, Toronto, 1914.

Anderson, Fred. *Crucible of War: The Seven Years' War and the Fate of Empire in British North America, 1754-1766.* Alfred A. Knopf, New York, 2000.

Beattie, Daniel J.; Maarten Ultee, editor. "The Adaptation of the British Army to Wilderness Warfare, 1755-1763." In *Adapting to Conditions: War and Society in the Eighteenth Century.* The University of Alabama Press, Tuscaloosa, Alabama, 1986, pp. 56-83.

Bellico, Russell P. *Chronicles of Lake Champlain: Journeys in War and Peace.* Purple Mountain Press, Fleischmanns, New York, 1999.

_____. *Chronicles of Lake George: Journeys in War and Peace.* Purple Mountain Press, Fleischmanns, New York, 1995.

_____. *Sails and Steam in the Mountains: A Maritime and Military History of Lake George and Lake Champlain.* Purple Mountain Press, Fleischmanns, New York, 1992, extensively revised 2001.

Bougainville, Louis-Antoine de. *Adventures in the Wilderness: The American Journals of Louis Antoine de Bougainville, 1756-1760.* Translated and edited by Edward P. Hamilton. The University of Oklahoma Press, Norman, 1964.

Bouquet, Henry. *The Papers of Henry Bouquet, December 11, 1755, July 1765.* Edited by Donald H. Kent, Louis M. Waddell, and Autumn L. Leonard. The Pennsylvania Historical and Museum Commission, Harrisburg. Published in six volumes: 1951, 1972, 1976, 1978, 1984, 1994.

Cleland, Hugh. *George Washington in the Ohio Valley.* University of Pittsburgh Press, Pittsburgh, 1955.

Cuneo, John R. *Robert Rogers of the Rangers.*

-Oxford University Press, New York, 1959, hardcover.

-Richardson & Steirman, NY, 1987, hardcover.

-The Fort Ticonderoga Museum, Ticonderoga, NY, 1988, trade paperback.

_____. Personal Notes for *Robert Rogers of the Rangers.* Unpublished; original in the collections of the William L. Clements Library, University of Michigan, Ann Arbor, Michigan; copy in the author's collection.

Dunnigan, Brian Leigh. *Siege 1759: The Campaign Against Niagara.* The Old Fort Niagara Association, Inc., Youngstown, NY, 1996.

Eckert, Allen W. *Wilderness Empire.* Little, Brown and Company, Boston, 1969.

Forbes, John. *Writings of General John Forbes Relating to His Service in North America.* Compiled and edited by Alfred Procter James, Ph.D. The Collegiate Press, Manasha, Wisconsin, 1938.

Fortescue, Hon. J. W. *A History of the British Army: First Part—To the Close of the Seven Years' War,* Volume II. MacMillan and Co., Limited, London, 1899.

Fowler, Barney. *The Adirondack Album,* Volume Two. North Country Books, Utica, New York, 1980

Frazier, Patrick. *The Mohicans of Stockbridge.* University of Nebraska Press, Lincoln, 1992.

Fuller, Archelaus. "Journal, May-November 1758." In *The Bulletin of the Fort Ticonderoga Museum,* Volume XIII, Number 1, December 1970, pp. 5-17.

Furnis, James. "An Eyewitness Account by James Furnis of the Surrender of Fort William Henry, August, 1757." Edited by William S. Ewing. *New York History,* July 1961, pp. 307-316.

Gallup, Andrew, and Donald F.Shaffer, La Marine: *The French Colonial Soldier in Canada, 1754-1761.* Illustrations by Joseph E. Lee. Heritage Books Inc., Bowie, Maryland, 1992.

Gallup, Andrew, editor. *Memoir of a French and Indian War Soldier, "Jolicoeur" Charles Bonin.* Heritage Books, Inc., Bowie, Maryland, 1993.

Hagerty, Gilbert. *Massacre at Fort Bull: The DeLery Expedition Against the Oneida Carry, 1756.* Mowbray Company, Providence, Rhode Island, 1971.

Hargreaves, Major Reginald. *The Bloodybacks.* Walker and Company, New York, 1968.

Harper, Colonel J. R. *78th Fighting Frasers in Canada: A Short History of the Old 78th Regiment or Fraser's Highlanders, 1757-1763.* DEV-SCO Publications, Ltd., Laval, Quebec, Canada, 1966.

Hawks, Major John. *Orderly Book and Journal of Major John Hawks on the Ticonderoga-Crown Point Campaign Under Jeffery Amherst, 1769-1760.* The Society of Colonial Wars in the State of New York, 1911.

Katcher, Philip. *Armies of the American Wars, 1753-1815.* Hastings House, New York, 1975.

Knox, John, and Arthur G. Doughty, editor. *An Historical Journal of the Campaigns in North America for the Years 1757, 1758, 1759, and 1760.* Published in three volumes by The Champlain Society, Toronto, 1914; reprinted by Greenwood Press, New York, 1968.

Loescher, Burt Garfield. *The History of Rogers' Rangers,* Volume I: *The Beginnings, January 1755-April 6, 1758.* Published privately by the author, San Francisco, California, 1946.

_____. *The History of Rogers' Rangers,* Volume II: *Genesis—Rogers' Rangers—The First Green Berets: The Corps and the Revivals, April 6, 1758-December 24, 1783.* Published privately by the author, San Mateo, California, 1969.

_____. *The History of Rogers' Rangers,* Volume III: *Officers and Non-Commissioned Officers.* Published privately by the author, Burlingame, California, 1957.

London Chronicle/Universal Evening Post, November 23-25,1758. Original in the collections of the Fort Ticonderoga Museum.

MacLeod, D. Peter. *The Canadian Iroquois and the Seven Years' War.* Canadian War Museum Historical Publication No. 29, Dundurn Press, Toronto, 1996.

May, Robin, with illustrations by Gerry Embleton. *Wolfe's Army.* Osprey Publishing, Ltd., Berkshire, England, 1974. Revised edition, with new color plates and text revisions by Gerry Embleton, 1997.

Mayo, Lawrence Shaw. *Jeffery Amherst.* Longmans, Green and Company, New York, 1916.

McCulloch, Lieutenant Colonel Ian, CD, editor. " `Believe Us, Sir, This Will Impress Few People!': Spin-Doctoring, 18th Century Style." In *The Bulletin of the Fort Ticonderoga Museum,* Volume XI, Number 1, 1998, pp. 92-107.

_____, and Donald E. Graves, editor. "Like roaring lions breaking from their chains: The Battle of Ticonderoga, 8 July 1758." In *Fighting for Canada: Seven Battles 1758-1945,* Robin Brass Studio Inc., Toronto, 2000, pp. 23-80.

_____, "Within Ourselves . . . The Development of British Light Infantry in North America During the Seven Years' War." Published in *Canadian Military History,* Volume 7, Number 2, Spring 1998, pp. 41-55.

Moody, Thomas, and P. M. Woodwell, editor. *Diary of Thomas Moody: Campaign of 1760 of the French & Indian War.* The Chronicle Print Shop, South Berwick, Maine, 1976.

O'Callaghan, E. B., editor. *Documents Relating to the Colonial History of the State of New York, Procured in Holland, England and France, by John Romeyn Brodhead, Esq.* Albany, New York, 1856.

Pargellis, Stanley McCrory. *Lord Loudoun in North America.* Yale University Press, 1933. Reprinted by Archon Books, 1968.

_____. *Military Affairs in North America, 1748-1765: Selected Documents from the Cumberland Papers in Windsor Castle.* American Historical Association, 1936. Reprinted by Archon Books, 1969.

Parkman, Francis. *Montcalm and Wolfe: The Decline and Fall of the French Empire in*

North America. Collier-Macmillan Ltd. edition, London, 1962. Originally published in 1884.

Pond, Peter. "The Narrative of Peter Pond." Edited by Charles M. Gates. Reprinted in *Five Fur Traders of the Northwest*. Minnesota Historical Society, St. Paul, 1965, pp. 11-59.

Pouchot, Pierre, edited and annotated by Brian Leigh Dunnigan. *Memoirs on the Late War in North America Between France and England*. Translated by Michael Cardy. The Old Fort Niagara Association, Inc., Youngstown, New York, 1994.

Richards, Frederick B., L.H.D. *The Black Watch at Ticonderoga and Major Duncan Campbell of Inverawe*. Heritage Books, Inc., Bowie, Maryland, 1999.

Roberts, Kenneth. *Northwest Passage*: Volume II, Appendix. Doubleday and Company, New York, 1937. This special limited edition set consists of two volumes. The second volume contains much of the primary source material that Roberts used when writing his famous novel.

Rogers, Robert. Journals of Major Robert Rogers.

-London, 1765.

-Dublin, 1769.

-University Microfilms Facsimile Edition, Ann Arbor, Michigan, 1966.

-Readex Microprint Corporation, New Canaan, Connecticut, 1966.

-Dresslar Publishing, Bargersville, Indiana, 1997. Dublin Edition.

-Purple Mountain Press Ltd., Fleischmanns, New York, 2002. Annotated and illustrated edition, to which is added Rogers' Journal of the Siege of Detroit and other material. Annotations by Timothy J. Todish and original illustrations by Gary S. Zaboly.

Rogers, Robert J., U.E. *Rising Above Circumstances: The Rogers Family in Colonial America*. Sheltus and Picard Inc., Bedford, Quebec, Canada, 1999.

Reeder, Colonel Russell P. "Red" Jr. *The French & Indian War*. Vermont Heritage Press, Quechee, Vermont, and the Fort Ticonderoga Association, Ticonderoga, New York, 1997. Originally published in 1972.

Russell, Francis. *The French and Indian Wars*. American Heritage Publishing Company, New York, 1962.

Smith, Bradford. *Rogers' Rangers and the French and Indian War*. Random House, New York, 1956.

Spicer, Abel; Russell P. Bellico, editor. "Journal for 1758." Reprinted in *Chronicles of Lake George: Journeys in War and Peace*, Purple Mountain Press Ltd., Fleischmanns, New York, 1995, pp. 91-119.

Stacey. C. P., *Quebec 1759: The Siege and the Battle*. Macmillan of Canada, Toronto, 1959.

Starbuck, David R. *The Great Warpath: British Military Sites from Albany to Crown Point*. University Press of New England, Hanover and London, 1999.

Stark, Caleb. *Memoirs and Official Correspondence of General John Stark*. Greg Press, Boston, 1972.

Steele, Ian K. *Betrayals: Fort William Henry & the "Massacre."* Oxford University Press, New York, 1990.

_____. *Warpaths: Invasions of North America.* Oxford University Press, New York, 1994.

Swartz, Seymour I. *The French and Indian War 1754-1763: The Imperial Struggle for North America.* Simon & Schuster, New York, 1994.

Todish, Timothy J. "Crown Point on Lake Champlain." In *Muzzleloader Magazine,* July/August 1984, pp. 45-49.

_____. Fortress Louisbourg: "The Gibraltar of North America." In *Muzzleloader Magazine,* May/June 1987, pp. 34-39.

_____. "Michilimackinac: Land of the Great Turtle." In *Muzzleloader Magazine,* March/April 1983, pp. 16-20.

_____. "Rangers at Fort Edward." In *Muzzleloader Magazine,* July/August 1990, pp. 54-58.

_____. "Rendezvous on the Ouabache: Fort Ouiatenon and the Feast of the Hunter's Moon." In *Muzzleloader Magazine,* September/October 1991, pp. 39-42

_____. "The 1758 Attack on Ticonderoga." In *Muzzleloader Magazine,* Part One, November/December 1999, pp. 54-61, and Part Two, January/February 2000, pp. 41-50.

_____. "Triumph and Tragedy: The Siege of Fort William Henry." In *Muzzleloader Magazine,* Part One, November/December 1992, pp. 36-40, and Part Two, pp. 31-36, January/ February 1993.

Waddell, Louis M., and Bruce D. Bomberger. *The French and Indian War in Pennsylvania: Fortification and Struggle During the War for Empire.* The Pennsylvania Historical and Museum Commission, Harrisburg, 1996.

Webster, Robert. "Robert Webster's Journal of Amherst's Campaign, April 5th to November 23rd, 1759." Original in the collections of the Fort Ticonderoga Museum. An edited version of this journal was published in *The Bulletin of the Fort Ticonderoga Museum,* Volume II, Number 4, July 1931.

West, Martin J., editor. *War for Empire in Western Pennsylvania.* The Fort Ligonier Association, Ligonier, Pennsylvania, 1993.

Westbrook, Nicholas, editor. " `Like Roaring Lions Breaking From Their Chains': The Highland Regiment at Ticonderoga." In *The Bulletin of the Fort Ticonderoga Museum,* Volume XVI, Number 1, 1998, pp. 16-91.

Windrow, Martin. *Montcalm's Army.* Osprey Publishing, Ltd., Berkshire, England, 1973.

Wolfe, Major General James. *Instructions to Young Officers and a Placart to the Canadians.* London, 1768. Museum Restoration Service Edition, Ottawa, Ontario, Canada, 1967.

Zaboly, Gary. "The Battle on Snowshoes." In *American History Illustrated,* December 1979, pp. 12-24.

_____. "Wilderness Commandos." In *Muzzle Blasts,* June 1978, pp. 7-14.

Acknowledgments

No author is ever solely responsible for the creation of a work. It is inevitable that he must draw upon the ideas and efforts of others while developing his manuscript into finished form. One of the most rewarding aspects of writing this book has been that it has caused me to bring into perspective the contributions of the many people who have helped me accumulate the information presented here. Not only have they all had an impact on the content of this book, I am proud to say that most of them are also my personal friends.

To attempt to name everyone whose knowledge influenced and assisted me would be an impossibility, but the following persons have played such a big part that to fail to recognize their contributions would be an injustice.

The book had its beginning as a slide program that I prepared for the Michigan Company of Military Historians and Collectors. It is only fitting that I begin my thanks by recognizing that fine group of gentlemen, whose purpose is not to glorify war, but rather to study it and learn from its lessons.

Special thanks are due to the fine artists who allowed me to reproduce their artwork in this book: Gary Zaboly, of New York City, who also generously shared his wealth of historical knowledge; Joe Lee, of Garden City, Michigan; and Tim Carlson, of Traverse City, Michigan.

I am also very grateful to the following people who helped in the preparation of the manuscript. Barbi Lensing of Grand Rapids, Michigan, did the manuscript typing for me. The following were kind enough to review the draft manuscript of this revised edition: Neal Burdick of Canton, New York, Associate Director of Communications for St. Lawrence University; Lieutenant Colonel Ian McCulloch, C.D., and his wife, Susan A. Johnson-McCulloch (formerly assistant director of Fort Ticonderoga), of Ottawa, Ontario, Canada; Dr. Todd Harburn of the Michilimackinac Society Press, Okemos, Michigan; Christopher Matheney, site director of the State-House Education and Visitor Center, Columbus, Ohio; and Nicholas Westbrook, executive director of Fort Ticonderoga, New York.

The following people have been valuable in helping me accumulate and understand the wide range of material presented in this book, most of them over a period of many years: Dr. David Armour, of Mackinac State Historic Parks, Michigan; Dr. Russell P. Bellico, of Feeding Hills, Massachusetts; George Alfred Bray III, of Rochester, New York; Brian Leigh Dunnigan, of the William L. Clements Library, Ann Arbor, Michigan; Gerry Embleton, of Preles, Switzerland; William Farrar, of the Crown Point State Historic Site, New York; Christopher Fox, of Fort Ticonderoga, New York; Greg Furness, formerly of the Crown Point State Historic Site, New York; Gary Foreman of Valparaiso, Indiana; Richard and JoAnne Fuller, of Fort Edward, New York; John C. Jaeger, of Flat Rock, Michigan; Robert Lancaster, of Croton, Michigan; Father Barry Lewis, of Corunna, Michigan; Scott Mann, of Laingsburg, Michigan; Thomas McElroy, of North Branch, Michigan; Frank J. Nastasi, of Muttontown, New York; John-Eric Nelson of Milford, Connecticut; David Nixon of Ludington, Michigan; Jerry Olson, of Dearborn, Michigan; Ian Pedler, of Bristol, England; Paul and Marjo Prinzing, of Muskegon, Michigan; Ray and Carole Rewold, of Alanson, Michigan; Robert J. Rogers, of St. Albert, Alberta, Canada; Jerry Shoger, of Fairfield, California; Tana Shoger-Vance, of Aurora, Illinois; Dr. David R. Starbuck, of Chestertown, New York; Timothy Titus, formerly of the Crown Point State Historic Site, New York; Terry Todish, of Grand Rapids, Michigan; Michael Tracy, of Mackinaw City, Michigan; and Dr. Keith Widder, of Lansing, Michigan.

Last, but not least, I would like to thank my publishers, Wray and Loni Rominger, of Purple Mountain Press, for having enough confidence in this book to send it into a second edition, and my high school history teacher, Mr. Jacob Robinson, of Grand Rapids, who nurtured my love of history, and is responsible for much of my knowledge of the technical aspects of historical research.

—Timothy J. Todish

Index

When possible, all persons are listed by full name, unit, and highest rank attained during the war. Where a page number is followed by a lower case "n," it indicates that the reference is in a footnote at the bottom of the page.

About the Author

TIMOTHY J. TODISH, a native of Grand Rapids, Michigan, has had a nearly lifelong interest in Rogers' Rangers and the French and Indian War. He is a graduate of Michigan State University with a degree in Management.

While still in college, Todish became interested in black powder shooting and historical reenacting, which still occupies much of his time. He is the Adjutant of the French and Indian War reenactment group Jaeger's Battalion, Rogers' Rangers.

Now retired from the Grand Rapids Police Department with over 27 years of service, Todish works as an independent historical writer and consultant, specializing in the French and Indian War and Alamo periods. He provided background information and worked as an extra in the 1992 movie *The Last of the Mohicans*, and also served as the technical advisor and appeared as an extra in the award-winning History Channel documentary *Frontier: Legends of the Old Northwest*. He has also done consulting for such productions as the Learning Channel show *Archaeology*, and the PBS series *Anyplace Wild*. Todish has written articles for a number of historical publications, and is on the Special Features staff and is a regular contributor to *Muzzleloader* magazine. In addition to his books, he has written a number of historical articles for such magazines as *The Journal of the Forces of Montcalm & Wolfe, Living History, Smoke & Fire News* and *F&I War*.

Praise for the First Edition of America's *First* First World War

"Like Rogers, this author (like many recreators) sees straight to the heart of the matter. And this author is much more readable by today's standards than Rogers. A book by a recreator, for fellow recreators—a splendid capsule of America's first, First World War." —*Living History Magazine*

"The book is that rare combination—absorbing yet scholarly. While you are anxious to see what happens next, each year of the war starts with a brief analysis of what the leaders hoped to accomplish that year, and by what strategy. The important part played by Rogers' Rangers is shown in much detail …There are interesting side-lights, even a ghost story known on both sides of the Atlantic." —*The Backwoodsman Magazine*

"Anyone who is interested in the French and Indian War would do well to order a copy of Timothy J. Todish's new book…" —*Muzzleblasts Magazine*

Other important books on the colonial period
published by Purple Mountain Press

by Robert Rogers, edited and annotated
by Timothy J. Todish and illustrated by Gary Zaboly
*The Annotated and Illustrated
Journals of Major Robert Rogers*

by Russell P. Bellico
*Sails and Steam in the Mountains: A Maritime and
Military History of Lake George and Lake Champlain*

Chronicles of Lake George: Journeys in War and Peace

Chronicles of Lake Champlain: Journeys in War and Peace

by Shirley W. Dunn
The Mohicans and Their Land, 1609-1730

The Mohican World, 1680-1750

by Theodore G. Corbett
*A Clash of Cultures on the War Path of Nations:
The Colonial Wars in the Hudson-Champlain Valley*

by Guy Omeron Coolidge
The French Occupation of the Champlain Valley

by Peter S. Palmer
History of Lake Champlain, 1609-1814

For a free catalog of these and other titles, write Purple Mountain
Press, Ltd., P.O. Box 309, Fleischmanns, NY 12430-0309, or call
845-254-4062, or fax 845-254-4476, or email purple@catskill.net.
http://www.catskill.net/purple